D1180585

*Love Letters of
the Great War*

Love Letters of
the Great War

Edited by Mandy Kirkby

MACMILLAN

First published 2014 by Macmillan
an imprint of Pan Macmillan, a division of Macmillan Publishers Limited
Pan Macmillan, 20 New Wharf Road, London N1 9RR
Basingstoke and Oxford
Associated companies throughout the world
www.panmacmillan.com

ISBN 978-0-230-77283-0

Contents

III. SEPARATION AND LONGING

IV. APRÈS LA GUERRE

V. SILVER LININGS   98

VI. THE LONGEST GOODBYE   128

VII. DARK DAYS   140

VIII. THE END OF THE WAR 176

List of Illustrations

Foreword

In December 1914, the largest wooden structure in the world was erected by the Post Office, within Regent's Park. This was the London Home Depot, where bags of mail for troops on the Western Front were sorted. It covered five acres and employed thousands of Post Office workers.

We understand that the First World War was fought on a scale and in a style never before seen; what is perhaps less familiar is the complex, sophisticated infrastructure that made such warfare feasible. The war became its own world, with its own hospitals, army schools and transport system, its own courts, prisons, workshops and communications. New technology and systems developed quickly under the pressure of need.

The efficient delivery of letters and parcels to serving soldiers was given high priority. On the Western Front, in particular, the static nature of trench warfare and established lines of communication made it possible for post to be delivered with startling rapidity. Again and again, letters home describe perishable food received in good – or fairly good – condition. In fact, as William Munton writes to his wife on

Boxing Day 1916 from 'Somewhere in France', the postman has praised her packing of the parcel: 'If everybody packed their parcels like that there would be less bad language used at the post office.' Close to twenty thousand bags of mail crossed the Channel each day.

As this collection of love letters makes clear, the same longing for letters, the same acute desire for a taste or touch of home, were expressed wherever the war penetrated. In Turkey, France, Italy, Russia, the USA, Germany and all the countries of the British Empire, husbands, wives and sweethearts devoted hours of thought to the post. To and fro went tunic buttons, photographs, picture postcards, soap, tins of ointment, oranges, OXO cubes, poems, pastries, and, above all, words that struggled to link the lives severed by war.

For as long as it took to read or write a letter, a soldier might think himself back into the world of home. Tired of 'so much masculine companionship', Captain W. D. Darling sends a few lines to his wife, telling her that his love for the 'freedom and camaraderie' of camp life has turned to hatred in the light of his longing to 'play with you, fondle you, and then seduce you'. Within a single letter, a soldier describes the beauty of the moon in its fleece of cloud, and lists what he needs in his next parcel from home: candles, rice and potted meat. Lovers write of dreams and desires, fears, depressions, the contrivances of their daily lives, faith and separation, and endless, endless waiting. Sometimes they are amusingly practical: 'I am getting more and more excited at the thought of seeing you on Tuesday. What are we going to do with Mother? We <u>must</u> lose her sometimes!' Letters may take the writer back 'to the old sweetheart days', but sometimes they are cries of agony, as when Amy Handley writes to Private John George Clifton: '– My heart – Surely it will burst – Jack – Jack – I want you –'. Tender, earthy, heart-rending, ardent, crammed with news, humour, rage and longing, the love-letters collected in this anthology bring to life a lost world.

One of the most poignant messages is one dropped into the English Channel in a ginger beer bottle by Private Thomas Hughes, on his way to France in September 1914. The simplicity of the note, which is sent 'just to see if it will reach you', is striking. This doubt about whether or not written words will 'reach' those for whom they are meant is common to many writers of the love letters here. There is anxiety that long absence will destroy the mutual understanding from which the relationship grew. There is the painful awareness that words are no substitute for touch, and that even the most lyrical, erotic evocation of the loved one's body will not bring it an inch closer. Above all, there is the fear of death, and final separation. Often, the foreboding was justified. Gunner Frank Bracey wrote to his sweetheart, Win, in May 1916: 'I am writing this because I have a feeling that I shall not come back again. You may think I am a bit taped writing this dear but I cannot help it. If I do come back dearest you will never see this letter but I have a strong feeling today that I shall never see England again . . . My last wish is that you marry a good man and to be happy and to think of your Humble now and then.' He was killed in action on the Western Front three months later.

Like Gunner Bracey, many of these letter writers show poignant humility about their own fate. Fears for themselves are over-ridden by the desire that those they love should 'be happy'. Soldiers downplay physical hardship, pain, danger and self-doubt; wives and sweethearts downplay loneliness, poverty or the difficulties of coping alone with home and children. But sometimes the struggle to protect the beloved from the rawness of the writer's experience is overwhelmed by a greater need to share it. Gunner Wilfrid Cove writes to his wife Ethel a compelling description of the shattered villages among which he is fighting. He asks her to imagine that she is standing in her own village, 'say where the pillar-box is', among shell-holes 'big enough to hold a couple of large motor omnibuses', in a landscape where 'every single thing upon it is directly appertaining to war'. However, eloquent though he is, Cove knows he cannot – and perhaps should not – 'adequately describe' the world in which he now finds himself. He ends with a paragraph about the 'excellent to the last' sausage rolls that Ethel has sent, and reassures her that her wrist-watch is still 'going strong' under bombardment. Home and 'somewhere in France', domesticity and industrialized warfare, are just about held in balance in this letter. Private Maurice Drans, however, describes to his fiancée Georgette Clabault the overwhelming horror of 'an open mine of innumerable scattered corpses without tombs, a mass grave open to the crawling worms . . . violated naked flesh.'

Official censorship, as well as intuitive self-censorship, must be borne in mind when reading these letters. In Britain, the Defence of the Realm Act 1914 legislated for the censorship of private correspondence from soldiers at the front. Junior officers read the men's letters and stamped them as censored. The Post Office also carried out censorship of soldiers' mail at base camps. The letters in this collection, intimate and revealing as they appear, were written in the knowledge that other eyes than the addressee's might read them. Privacy is one more casualty of the war, but many correspondents ignore that fact. They write as if their private loves were still supreme and inviolable, and perhaps they had good reason. The war could take everything from them, at any moment. A few words scribbled before a trench raid might be all that would survive to convey their love.

Helen Dunmore, October 2013

Introduction

A great many of the letters in this book have never been published before and have been dug out of archives and brought into the light of day for the first time in decades. Researching original material is a time-consuming business, and finding these love letters has involved many hours of trawling through what are called 'Private Papers'. These are the documents relating to an individual's wartime experience, donated to museums and archives, usually by a relative once the original recipient has died. The contents of Private Papers can be very varied and truly surprising, anything from service records and notifications of death to army-issue French phrase books, leave passes and, of course, personal letters home – to parents and friends, to wives and sweethearts.

Some preliminary legwork has already been done for the researcher in the form of the archivist's catalogue entries. These follow certain conventions, however, carefully and objectively describing the items in the Papers, and only sometimes is there a hint of the true nature of what lies within. A collection of letters might be described as 'poignant' or 'personal' but this doesn't really express how fiery or eloquent, intimate or magical the contents might turn out to be.

Research rooms in archives and museums tend to be very similar – low lighting, plain and simple surroundings, temperature-controlled, practical and suited to the purpose. You sit in your allotted place and wait for the requested material to be brought up from the storeroom. Then the box arrives. Inside, cardboard folders tied with cotton ribbon hold letters and documents, but often there are other objects in the box, the flotsam and jetsam of a wartime life – delicate trinkets folded in tissue, a photograph album or an intriguingly bulky envelope – all treasures waiting to be revealed.

There were some objects that particularly thrilled and surprised me – a stationery set with its writing paper still inside, an officer's swagger stick ('the end chewed off by a dog', according to the note in the file), an embroidered silk postcard 'To My Darling', a leather wallet, a faded hand-kerchief, an envelope full of pieces of shrapnel (astonishingly heavy). Then there were the photographs, of handsome young men in uniform and demure-looking girls in their best dresses – and one in a locket, on the reverse of which was scribbled 'Only au revoir, beloved. Only au revoir'.

These mementoes and ephemera merely hint at what's to come: the letters are the real heart of the matter. They are such simple things, just paper and pencil and ink, many of them faded with age, but time and again I was bowled over by the wonderful and astonishing things people said in them, and under such terrible circumstances.

Occasionally, it felt odd to be reading such personal letters. I was a little embarrassed by Amy Handley's awful distress at being separated from Jack, and I felt I really shouldn't be reading the anonymous conscientious objector's erotic evocation of his lover, or Cicely Marriott's lovely little note to her husband telling him that they'd had a baby girl.

Friends often asked, 'Isn't it making you rather sad? Don't they all die in the end?' Well, no, they didn't all die in the end: many survived and their love was no doubt the stronger for it. Robert Block's joyous letter to his sweetheart written when peace was declared made me happy all day and very, very glad – like him – to be alive.

Yet it was hard not to feel emotional when faced with a very sad letter, and I frequently told myself off for being self-indulgent. After all, these things happened so long ago, it felt silly to be affected by them. And then I came across something in the Wilfrid Cove papers.

The file consisted of a small collection of letters between a husband, wife and young daughter, and in them, the warmth and closeness of this family was unmistakable. It was obvious early on that Wilfrid hadn't survived the war, and this was sad enough, but then right at the bottom of the archive box I saw a white envelope.

Out came a small, squashed block of letters and photographs merged together in a single mass, the edges all dirty and torn, and uppermost was a picture of a little girl in a fairy dress. It then became clear: Wilfrid had probably kept these letters and photographs in his tunic pocket and the squashed appearance and damage must have been from the impact of the shell that had killed him.

I was finding it quite hard to fight back the tears when I turned to the archivist's typed note from thirty or so years before, when the collection was first donated to the archive. As the usual practice dictated, the archivist had carefully outlined the contents, but this time he had added a few extra lines: 'Reading this record one feels one gets to know this living, lively family, and it is an emotional experience. The tragedy of Gunner Cove's death could not have happened to a nicer and closer family. I am privileged to have been "involved" infinitesimally in their lives.'

He too had been affected by the Cove family, and how could this not be so? It isn't foolish at all to be affected by long-past tragedies; we are human and, especially where love is concerned, we can't help but feel an emotional link going right back through the years.

Many of the sons and daughters of these long-ago lovers and letter writers are still alive, and for them, of course, the link is direct. In correspondence with these relatives, I was told the same story many times: they had had no idea of the existence of the letters, often no idea of the existence of the sweetheart who had been killed. It was only after the recipient had died that the correspondence came to light – ribbon-tied bundles found in the attic or hidden at the back of a drawer. 'My mother was very private' and 'We never knew' were very typical responses.

[xx]

These women had held on to their letters because their love was something wonderful that had happened to them, something worth preserving, even in secret. I hope that by bringing so many letters out from the archives, we can acknowledge these couples all over again and, like the Cove family archivist, have the privilege of being involved, albeit infinitesimally, in their love.

Mandy Kirkby, October 2013

*Love Letters of
the Great War*

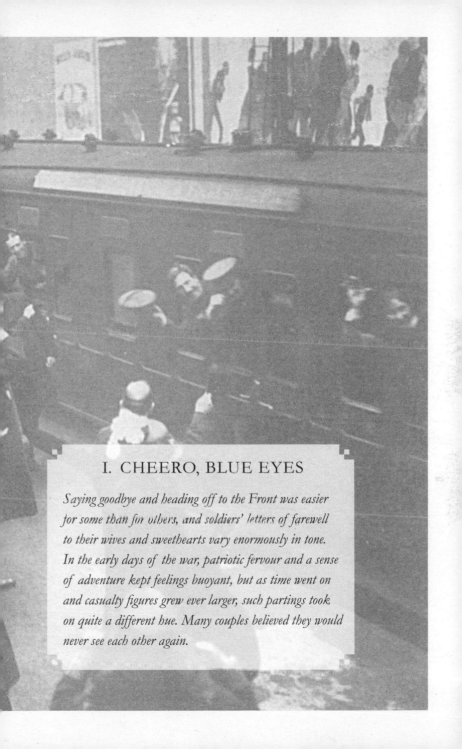

I. CHEERO, BLUE EYES

*Saying goodbye and heading off to the Front was easier
for some than for others, and soldiers' letters of farewell
to their wives and sweethearts vary enormously in tone.
In the early days of the war, patriotic fervour and a sense
of adventure kept feelings buoyant, but as time went on
and casualty figures grew ever larger, such partings took
on quite a different hue. Many couples believed they would
never see each other again.*

Corporal Alfred Chater to Joyce Francis

Alfred Chater was already a volunteer soldier with a London regiment when war broke out in August 1914. He was called up immediately for active service and, after three months' training, was sent to France. From his training camp, he sent a letter to his sweetheart on the eve of departure.

Oct 25th 1914
Trowley House
Abbots Langley

Darling Joy,

I must write you one more line dearest to say goodbye before we go, as god knows when I shall see you again. I am so awfully glad we are going – it is what we have been waiting for for so long and it has come so much sooner than we expected or hoped. I heard about it yesterday afternoon when I was going home; I called at our headquarters at Euston where I found the 2nd Battalion being got together and was told the 1st Btn were to leave for France on Monday. I think there is not much doubt that we are really going: we were served out with new rifles this afternoon and we believe that we shall be at Southampton tomorrow night.

I wish I could have seen you today and I can't bear the thought of going without saying goodbye to you but perhaps it is better as it is. So now dear it is goodbye and may we meet again if god wills. You know that if I am allowed to come back I shall feel exactly the same to you as I do now and shall be ready for you whenever you can come to me and you know that I shall come straight to you and ask you directly I come back.

It's a funny game this war! We are all fairly shouting with joy at going and I daresay we shall soon be cursing the day and then when we get back we shall say we have had the time of our lives. Goodbye darling, may god bless and keep you.

Goodbye little girl.

Micky

Lieutenant Geoffrey Boothby to Edith Ainscow

Geoffrey Boothby had only just met Edith Ainscow when he was sent to the Front where he served with the Royal Engineer Tunnellers. Edith was very young, only seventeen, and Geoffrey not much older at twenty. They had spent just four days together and theirs was very much a fledgling romance, which would, in part, account for the breezy tone of the letter.

8th S. Staffords

B.E.F.

France

Postmarked 26 July 1915

Darling,

You now have a real live 'lonely soldier somewhere in France'. Only he's not very lonely. Also it's beastly conceited to imagine you hadn't got several others. Let us say 'another – er – boy in France'. Also please forgive him, if he's not feeling depressed or homesick. He's not. Never been more excited in his life before.

You see we're waiting way back behind the firing line for our turn for a little amateur scrapping. Knowing you as I do (having been in your company for, I believe, a period of four incomplete days all told), knowing you as I do, I repeat, I feel certain you will condone this temporary lapse from heartbrokenness under which I am supposed to stagger.

Only once have I strafed the Germans for bringing me out here to make a nuisance of myself & that was when I got your telegram, which got here yesterday by the way.

However, it's not much use kicking up a row about it, Kitchener's not one of my intimates, so I'll have to pass it over this time & qualify to be a divinity by your method – forgiveness.

To come to some real news, we've had a mixed sort of time since we came out. Easy billets & some very mouldy marching.

The men stuck it damn well. We had a long march under the most trying conditions for some of them especially those with tender feet. The notorious pavé or cobbled roads are the last word. As usual our regt. came off easily best in marching, having two fall out against eighty-two of another regt. Some boys, ours. Grousing all the while, but sticking to it like Trojans. We are now within sound of the big guns & sight of aerial scraps, which seem to occur every evening. Haven't seen one brought down yet.

We have great fun getting the inhabitants to execute our wishes. I haven't been stumped yet, though I can't understand a word they answer. We have been issued with a blue book of useful sentences which strange to relate ARE useful. I stride into a new billet, rap out my stock phrase, <u>vide</u> book & thenceforward carry on with patchy sentences or scattered words. Works, though, you'ld be surprised at the powers of understanding these people have.

Well, I suppose we're fixtures here for a month or two. Happy Days!

Cheero, Blue Eyes,

Geoff

Lieutenant Erwin von Freiherr Pflanzer-Baltin to Violet Murchison

On the day Germany declared war on France, twenty-one-year-old Erwin von Freiherr Pflanzer-Baltin of the Austro-Hungarian army wrote to his English fiancée whilst on a train journeying towards Belorussia on the Eastern Front. Erwin's tone is very serious; he's certainly not rejoicing at the prospect of going to war. He is aware of the dangers he is about to face and it probably hasn't escaped his notice that, even if he survives, their relationship will be difficult to sustain, given that they are on opposing sides. He wishes he has a better photograph of Violet: 'I must make do with the little one, which I always have next to my heart and will have till I die.' Ten days later, he was killed in action.

Miss Violet Murchison
Wyke House
Isleworth
London
England

Journey to Galicia

My most dearly beloved Baby!

Don't be angry that I haven't written for so long, but now that we are at war there is so terribly much to do that I scarcely know whether I'm coming or going. On 1st August I became a lieutenant, and leaving my comrades was very hard and full of emotion, because they are all off to the war, and who knows whether we will ever see each other again. I can't write any better than this, because I am in a moving train. I wanted to join my regiment yesterday and was given orders to go to Göding to the 6th Squadron. I entrained my horses in Vienna and travelled to Göding. When I reached Göding everything was already entrained and the regiment left at 11.30 pm for the Russian frontier. I had to stay in Göding and wait for my horses, which were late and didn't arrive until 1.30 am. I then got into the horsebox with them and have spent all of last night and today there and have all of tonight, before I arrive tomorrow morning. War has reached me already as I am sleeping in the straw, and instead of going on leave to England to my beloved Baby I'm off to Russia, and God grant that we will see each other again. Pray for your Erwin: when he is in the greatest danger he will always think of you. It's a pity that you didn't give me a better photograph of yourself, so that I must make do with the little one, which I always have next to my heart and will have till I die.

I haven't heard from you for such a long time, my sweet Baby, please write to me at the front very very often. I shall let you know the address of the forces post office and then you can write to me. But don't be angry, my sweet darling, I shall never be able to tell you where I am or what I am doing, because that is classified and forbidden on pain of court-martial.

I shall send you word of me as often as I can, but if you don't hear anything from me for a long time, you will know that I have been killed for the Fatherland. Never stop thinking of your Erwin, and pray for him, for his thoughts are with you every moment and he will fight with all his heart with you in his thoughts, sweet Baby.

Write to me very often, for I am so unhappy that I might have to lose you and perhaps never be able to see you again. I think of you and kiss your little picture, and close my letter with the request to give your dear mother my heartfelt regards, and remain, embracing you tenderly with my warmest greetings and kisses, loving you for ever faithfully and sincerely, your

Erwin

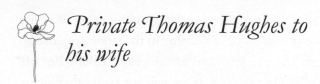

Private Thomas Hughes to his wife

On his way to France, twenty-six-year-old Thomas Hughes dropped a message in a green ginger beer bottle into the English Channel, addressed to his wife.

8/9 September 1914

Dear Wife,

I am writing this note on this boat and dropping it into the sea just to see if it will reach you. If it does, sign this envelope on the right hand bottom corner where it says receipt. Put the date and hour of receipt and your name where it says signature and look after it well. Ta ta sweet, for the present.

Your Hubby

xxx

The covering note says:

Sir or madam, youth or maid,

Would you kindly forward the enclosed letter and earn the blessing of a poor British soldier on his way to the front this ninth day of September, 1914.

Signed

Private T. Hughes,

Second Durham Light Infantry.

Third Army Corp Expeditionary Force.

Sergeant Major Giuseppe Castellani to Antonia Castellani

When Italy joined the war in April 1915, Giuseppe Castellani's younger brother was called up to join the army. Their mother was horrified and asked Giuseppe, who had served in the army in the Italo-Turkish War a few years earlier, to go in his place. This Giuseppe did, leaving his wife Antonia distraught. Two years later, they still find parting hard to bear.

19 September 1917

My Angel,

Last night I received a letter from you. I learned how strong was the pain on the day we had to separate. Do you remember those beautiful kisses? Do you remember the last one we gave each other between the tears? You did not dare to say a word. The tears were suffocating you. While passing by, you were at the window. The train guard also told me that. I didn't see you. I almost thought you didn't keep the promise made. I didn't dare to watch more than once. My poor heart was suffocated not by tears, but by a strong passion that I couldn't resist. You knew what my beliefs were. Also having to leave you again, what sorrow. By the end of the year we hope this will end.

Greetings and kisses

Giuseppe

Enjoy this souvenir from me. In these rough mountains you can find these flowers.

The mountain flower is an edelweiss.

Herbert Weisser to his sweetheart

We don't know very much about Herbert Weisser except that he was a student of architecture in Charlottenburg in Germany, and was killed in May 1915, in the Second Battle of Ypres, aged nineteen. There is much foreboding here, and it seems that Herbert is saying goodbye to himself as much as to his sweetheart. He is terribly conflicted, wanting to set her free but also wanting her to remember him for ever.

5th day of mobilization

Can you believe that now I sometimes cannot get away from the thought that I shall be killed? Then come quite close to me! I lay my hand upon your curly head and speak to you. Then I feel as if a God-given strength went out from me and as if all my wishes for you must be realized. Come, let me look deep into your eyes! I can see something burning there, but not for me; that is not necessary, really not. That fire must develop into a constant, steady flame, and that flame shall guide your children along the road that we have conquered together.

I stroke your hair gently, gently as one strokes the hair of the girl one loves, and I beg you not to forget all this; to remember all your life what we have been through together and to see that our efforts bear fruit. I wish, I most heartily wish, that your future may be as full of sunshine as you yourself can picture it; that you may some day have a son, with blue far-seeing eyes, firmly fixed on a distant goal, who will grow tall and slim, with a noble brow and finely cut nostrils – can you guess where he will get all that from? And then, you know, it is not impossible that he may become an architect. Then you will tell him all about our German cathedrals and show him what real German master-builders have created; how German architecture demonstrates an appreciation of what is grand and, at the same time, simple; of all that is honest, logical and strong; how it sends rays of light all over the world and how these rays are reflected back into the heavens in aspirations after the ideal. And then show him that man's whole interior life can also be full of beauty and sunshine if, instead of suppressing his own gifts, he perfects and ennobles them.

See, these are the things that I am thinking about before I go to the Front. And I am convinced that I could accomplish far more for the Fatherland along the lines in which I have already begun, and later on could produce much as the result of what I have absorbed during my youth. But we must not think of that now. Our present task is to defend all that German culture has built up through a thousand years of work, in toil and sweat and blood. But one would be glad to leave some trace behind one when one disappears from this world. You are the one who, during all our professional studies and also otherwise in life, has stood closest to me and on whom my personality has had most influence, even if you were perhaps not the one whom I loved best – that you know – and if I am killed you must carry on my life with your own. We can no longer believe in a life beyond the grave, but we can survive in our works, which are chiefly preserved in our friends, and perhaps you will find a life's companion who will help you in this.

My thoughts give me no peace, they carry me again and again to you.

Private Wellington Murray Dennis to Margaret Munro

Murray Dennis and Margaret Munro were both from the city of Stratford in Ontario, Canada, and were engaged when Murray enlisted in April 1916. They wrote to each other regularly and although Murray says in this letter, sent from England en route to France, 'I'm not lonesome nor downhearted', not a single postcard or letter sent to Margaret (including this one) could convince otherwise. He is completely downcast, and not even the experience of being in a foreign country can alleviate his homesickness. 'We had thought to be living our lives together and at peace,' he says in another letter. 'Funny how Fate plays tricks with human plans.'

Y.M.C.A. and
Canadian War Contingent Association
With the Canadian Forces

4 May 1917

Dear Mar.

Just got back from a four mile route march. We passed by Bramshott church. It is very old, some say 1107. It is all covered with ivy. And as soon as I get a chance I'll get a snap of it. The houses are very much different from Ontario and the roads flanked with hedges. There are no able bodied civilians around here and in fact no one but old people. The country is surely pretty. Still there is no country like 'my ain country' and no girl like my own.

No, I'll not forget to write dear and I'll never forget the few minutes we have had together at S.F. I'm not lonesome nor downhearted but I'm surely thinking of you and what might have been had this war not intervened. Still we were wise that we did not marry, no matter what our hearts prompted. The cause is worthy and I don't regret the sacrifice except for your sake.

Well dear girl I will close with love from

Murray

From Private Vasily Mishnin's Diary

Vasily Mishnin was from Penza in central Russia. He was twenty-seven years old and newly married to Nyura, who was already pregnant when he was conscripted into the army. It was more than a year since war broke out, and there had been heavy losses on the Russian side; Vasily might very well have been taking a train to certain death. This description of their leavetaking is from his diary.

25 December 1915

The first bell – a shiver runs through my whole body. We take our places in the carriages. Pushing and shoving. Some are drunk, some sober. Everyone is clambering around the carriage. This doesn't feel like the right time to be saying goodbye, perhaps for ever.

The third whistle. Everybody breaks down. Loud crying, hysterics, whole families weeping. I kiss my Nyura for the last time and all of my family kiss me. I can hardly hold back the tears. I say goodbye to Nyura. She shouts, 'Why are you crying, Vasiusha, you said you weren't going to cry!' Beside myself, I climb into the carriage with the rest and look at the crowd. I can hear wailing, and a tumult of voices, but I've suddenly gone numb. My nerves are in shreds. I gaze at the pitiful crowd, but then my eyes find Nyura again and everything changes. I want to jump out of the carriage and kiss her again, for the last time. Too late, the long whistle of the steam train screams out, it's ready to separate us from our loved ones and take us – God knows where. I am about to climb out of the carriage, when something stirs under my feet. I feel the train moving. The crowd is whipped up into a yet more violent state of hysteria. My heart pounds as the carriage rolls on. We will perhaps never return to Penza.

We are pulled away from the doors and they are locked shut. Someone starts up our favourite tune, 'Today Must Be Our Final Day', to take our minds off all this, but I huddle up in a corner. The song upsets me so much, it is hard to compose myself. I feel ashamed. While my comrades sing, I can't stop crying, can't calm down.

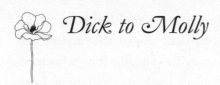

Dick to Molly

We don't know the exact circumstances surrounding this brief note, posted before the writer left for France. A Reverend Pat McCormick, a chaplain who censored the letters of his regiment, recalled it with some amusement and quotes it in his memoir of the war. Whether this was a fleeting relationship or the beginnings of a serious one, we shall never know.

Dear Molly,

A Happy Christmas. I am sending this to my aunt to forward to you as I do not know the address. Please tell me your name as I have forgotten it.

    Yours,

        Dick

II. SOMEWHERE IN FRANCE

Soldiers on active service were forbidden to disclose their whereabouts and so, when writing home, they would often put 'Somewhere in France' at the top of a letter in place of a real address. This was, of course, a witty comment on the circumstances of war, but its vagueness sums up perfectly the situation couples found themselves in – hundreds of miles apart and never knowing when it would all end. The Army Postal Service, on all sides in the conflict, performed miracles in keeping loved ones in touch, and conveyed millions of letters, postcards, parcels of home comforts and love tokens to and from the Front.

Gunner William Munton to Nellie Munton

From their letters, it's clear that William and Nellie Munton had a close and loving marriage, and they both made great efforts to sustain it during their wartime separation. William sent Nellie long, solicitous letters and little poems, which he dedicated to her, and Nellie responded with a stream of packages packed with comforts and useful things. Christmas must have been a particularly difficult time for them, when thoughts of home came sharply into focus, but they coped with it in typical fashion. For William though, the parcel of seasonal treats must have been a lifeline.

Boxing Day
Dec 26/16

(You can send me another tin of Boracic ointment. It's very useful!!)

My Dear Nellie,

It is Boxing Day but what a strange one, still I have had as good a Christmas as circumstances will permit. We are on the move again but not for long this time. You would like to know how I spent Xmas Day of course. Well I spent about four hours of it walking up and down a country lane 'Somewhere in France' waiting for the dump to come up. We got there at 10.30 & the dump didn't come until 2.30. I suppose the motor drivers stopped to have their Christmas dinner before they came along. However I didn't mind so very much because I had my parcel & it couldn't have come better than on Christmas Day, could it. It was packed very wisely and well, in fact just how I would expect my sensible little wife to pack it. It was in splendid condition & the postman who happened to stand by when I opened it said 'If everybody packed their parcels like that there would be less bad language used at the post office.' And what a fine parcel it was too. I had some fare on Christmas Day after all & let me say Darling that the value of the contents was greatly enhanced by the simple phrase that this was your Christmas Box. God Bless you Darling, I only wish that I could be at home to say all I would like to.

I want you to know that I am always thinking about you, ay dreaming about you & longing to be back with you again. God hasten the end of the war & shorten these days of suffering & of pain. I commend you to His loving care & keeping constantly, & know that you in turn are praying for me. Continue to do so Nellie Dear. 'More things are wrought by prayer than this world dreams of' & perhaps as you anticipate peace is a little nearer at hand, God will end this bloodshed & slaughter.

Goodbye Darling & God always Bless You with all the Love of my being.

Your affectionate husband

Will xxxxxxxx

A New Year Wish

For the opening of another year
I'd wish you joy & gladness
But that I know these days of stress
Bring sorrow, pain & sadness.
And so instead, I'm wishing you
A New Year filled with peace,
And trust in the Eternal God,
And faith that shall not cease.

I'm glad you like my bits of poetry, they are most of them original. This is, so was the verse on your Xmas card & also the little poem you evidently liked 'The link of Husband & wife'. I pass the time away composing little verses.

God Bless You Love

Gunner Wilfrid Cove to Ethel Cove

Wilfrid Cove enlisted in 1916, leaving behind his wife and two young daughters in the family home in Harrow in Middlesex. That they were a loving family is very apparent from the collection of letters left behind. Alongside Wilfrid's letters to Ethel are preserved those he wrote to his eldest daughter, Marjorie, and hers to him in return, which she had decorated with drawings of fairies.

In this letter to Ethel, he tries to convey something of his experiences to her; he really wants her to see what he can see. His description of the battlefield is intricate and affecting – and then, in one great leap, he rounds off his letter with a lightness of touch and a word of thanks for the 'excellent sausage rolls'. The contrast seems strange and a little amusing perhaps, but how else is he to cope with what is happening to him if not to attempt a return to normality once in a while?

Tuesday Nov 14th 1916

My Darling Ethel,

I hope by now you have received my birthday present, but in case you haven't here's again wishing you many many happy returns of your birthday. It is the first of your birthdays that we have been apart since you were sweet seventeen that I can remember. I hope and trust it will be the last.

Heaven send that by your next birthday – or mine come to that – this terrible war will be over & that we may both be spared & united on each of our birthdays and those of our dear little kiddies & for many years to come. I had a letter from your mother yesterday & she speaks of you as being wonderfully brave and cheerful under the circumstances. I am sure no man realizes more than I do what a brave & good wife I am blessed with and I thank God for it. Your bravery has been proved more than once and your goodness has always been apparent and if I am spared to survive this war, I will do my earnest endeavour to make myself worthy of you.

It causes me many regrets and much sorrow when I remember that my selfishness has more than once caused you unhappiness and I sincerely hope that my future conduct will make you realize that notwithstanding my shortcomings I do love you with all my heart and I do realize that I have one of the best wives in the world. I can now quite understand the Late Lord Kitchener's preference for bachelors as soldiers. He must have realized, altho a bachelor himself, that it is not the coward's fear of death but the fear that by death many a good soldier may thus be prevented from rejoining the wife & family he loves so much. I have just that very feeling myself at times when the shells are dropping all around us and the air is whistling with them.

This morning another terrific bombardment started from our guns. It is impossible for me to adequately describe it but I will endeavour to picture it to you. You must imagine that you are standing on say where the pillar-box is. Wealdstone you must suppose was once a little village by itself – also Headstone, Greenhill & Pinner – with houses built in the true village style, not in batches. These villages are now heaps of bricks and bits of roofs – absolutely nothing more – not a wall standing anywhere. Great holes big enough to hold a couple of large motor omnibuses, caused by bursting shells, are almost touching, and a party of men can only thread their way in single file along the ridges between them. Continual rains have made these into little lakes, in some cases with 4 to 6 feet of water in them. The lovely trees on Marlboro Hill, or Bushey Common away to Pinner are nothing more than stumps ranging from 3 to 10 feet. A few – a very few – have managed to save themselves from being broken in two – and these are only doing so by a bit of bank – the trunk having fallen over and resting on the trunks of others. The roads here are more like cart tracks over muddy fields. Everywhere as far as the eye can reach is barren & desolate & every single thing upon it is directly appertaining to war. Every man, every cart or wagon, every telephone wire – even in the very air one only sees aeroplanes – the birds having, I suppose, quitted long since to more peaceful climes – all is to one purpose. You must now imagine that in the rear vicinity one can see huge guns in a line & in lines one behind the other. These lines disappear from view with the broken and devastated woods. You might be standing on the site of the old pillar-box, when – crash go the guns all around at the same second. You look around & far away to Bushey you see the guns belching out huge flames & volumes of smoke in quick succession – and you realize that there are more guns than one could see before. The earth veritably trembles & the shells from the many batteries behind you rush over through the air, screaming & whistling according to their size & altitude. You turn to speak to a friend but the noise compels you to shout into his ear if you want to make yourself heard. This poor description will give you some idea of a bombardment. I must leave you to imagine it from a German point of view! It is a marvel if even one escapes such a hail.

Weds November 15th

I finished up your sausage rolls tonight. Excellent to the last. The box is just what I wanted. Thanks to vigilant searches, water, soap and the Powder, am now quite free of those horrible insects, thank goodness. Your watch is still going strong & has become the watch of the cellar & detachment. 'What's the time, Cove?' is the order of the day. Will close tonight, darling, & tumble in. It is late (9.45) & I'm writing these few lines after a good game of chess by a candle which reminds me that 'time's up'. Goodnight my darling. Longing and hoping for a letter from you tomorrow. Xxxx

In this lovely little letter from Wilfrid to his daughter Marjorie (overleaf), you can sense that, once again, he was striving to maintain a sense of normality. He clearly cherished her letters and drawings, which he used to decorate the walls of his dug-out.

Gunner Wilfrid Cove to Marjorie Cove

Monday Dec 4th 1916

My dear little Marjorie,

I have only just received your little letter which Mamma sent with hers on Nov 19th. Do you remember that you asked me to be home for Xmas? I only wish I could but there are many more soldiers in our Battery who are more entitled to the Xmas leave than I am, so am afraid you will have to do without Daddy this Xmas. Santa Claus will come just as usual. Will you tell Mamma that I will remember the old family custom at 20c on Xmas day. I think your writing and dictation just splendid, and your drawings are getting funnier than ever. I have pinned your crayoned tulips on the wall of my dug-out bedroom just beside your photograph. I wish you could see Daddy's bedroom. I'm sure you would laugh very much. It is dug out of the ground. The walls are made of filled sand bags. It has a nice wooden floor, the roof is iron & on top is earth with grass growing on it! I can just stand upright in the middle and without banging my head. Daddy is as comfortable as possible & I expect that even you would get tired enough to go soundly asleep in this dug-out. It would certainly be a change from your pink bedroom.

And how is little Daffodil getting on? I expect you quite enjoy the time when Mamma reads you more about her. It was Mamma's book when she was a little girl like you. Write again soon, dear, & send another crayoning to help cover the sand bags.

Heaps of love & kisses, which you must share with Mamma and Betty.

From your ever loving Daddy

One of Marjorie's pretty letters.

Wilfrid kept this photograph of his daughters, along with the letter from Marjorie on the previous page, close to his heart. They were both found in his breast pocket when he was killed in 1917.

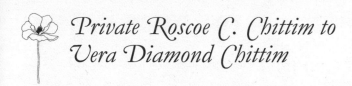

Private Roscoe C. Chittim to Vera Diamond Chittim

Roscoe C. Chittim was conscripted into the American army in June 1918. He had been married for just a year to the daughter of wealthy parents, and neither Vera nor Roscoe bore their enforced separation gracefully. Vera's letters to her husband are affectionate, but his in return are quite different. Instead of writing a love letter, he takes the opportunity to gripe and moan. Does he miss her at all, the reader can't help wondering, or does he just miss his comfortable American life?

Somewhere in France, Nov. 6, 1918, and believe me if you could see this place you would believe the above heading. I don't even know where we are, only France.

Dearest Little Wife,

Some time perhaps I can tell you about this letter and you may appreciate it more than you do now. I walked about eight miles in a driving rain and under conditions that a year ago I would not have thought possible, to get this paper and it cost enough to make one stagger. I am laying on my stomach in a bunch of straw soaking wet and so am I. My shelter tent is leaking all over and I have about two inches of candle for my heat. It has been raining for two days and nights so you can possibly imagine some of the pains we have.

I have had no mail yet and don't know when to expect any but some time it will get started to us. But we have been moving so fast since we came here. We were only in England a very few days after we landed at Liverpool. We went to Knotty Ash a camp near there then moved across England and came here. The people there are very enthusiastic over the Sammies as they call us. The French are more quiet and hard hit by the war, but cheerful and know that the future is bright for them. You do not see any men in uniform unless they are ex-soldiers or old men.

Things can't adjust over here as much as they do at home and some times never, and the very things we want we cannot get – sweets of any kind, matches and such small things. But the Kaiser will pay for it all. I would like to have that guy out here tonight in this rain and mud. Believe me he will get his and then some for all that we boys have to stand, and there will never be any let up till they quit absolutely.

You have read of sunny France well it isn't. But I suppose that is caused from the shell shock in the atmosphere or some other cause. My French vocabulary is getting quite large. I know several words and can make signs to beat the band. All over France you see hundreds of signs 'Café', and you go in to get something to eat, but can't: it's vin and such stuff any one that could drink it has an excellent taste for vinegar. I tryed it to see what it was like but never again, and the reason is I guess is shortage of sugar.

You can try nice grapes some places (not here) if you have enough money, they are very high. I have plenty of money but it does no good just now. However, I guess I will be out some as they say, they are not very prompt about paying the men here but if they get to a base some place they get it.

Not long ago an hour or so a new bunch of men came in from a long march with packs soaking wet and I can hear them yelling out there in the rain trying to get something dry but that's impossible, something to sleep on or such. Poor devils it's tough but they are all yelling and laughing, kidding each other. Other places you can hear boys singing, cussing, yelling and once in a while 'Damn the Kaiser'.

We men all fed tonight on <u>slum</u> and coffee. What slum is I don't quite know but it's meat and a lot of stuff mixed in a sort of soup form. Get over here dear as the little cook – But no joking you could do well out here even if you only knew how to boil water for a time.

Believe me I would like to be with you tonight in our own dining room with old Van waiting on us with a big steak about a yard long and everything that goes with it.

Well baby girl I'll tell you good night early, hit the hay because I'll need some sleep. It's now 7.30 p.m. about 1.30 in Dallas. I wonder where you are. Be sweet and oceans of love to you and also to mother dad aunt sis, everybody in fact I think of you all.

Good night, your loving husband, Ros.

Maria to Lieutenant Commander Anselm Lautenschlager

We don't know very much at all about this couple, certainly nothing about Maria, but we do know that Anselm Lautenschlager was serving with the German High Seas Fleet on board the battleship SMS Emden. Maria writes this letter in May 1919, more than six months since the Armistice, and Anselm still hasn't returned home. The relaxed tone of the letter is palpable. She knows he will return, it's just a matter of when, but nevertheless she still needs to write and affirm the link, and she uses her imagination to bring him closer.

Essen

31 May 1919

Good evening, dear Anselm,

I've already sent off a letter this morning, but when I am quite alone at home I always have to come to you. Father has gone out this evening, and Bibi is going to bed, so I'll quickly come for a little to my dear Anselm. So now I'm with you in spirit on the 'Emden', I'm sure you're just having a stroll on deck and I'll come with you. Sadly I'm rather late, so I've missed the sunset which I'm sure was splendid, but it doesn't matter, it's nice just being with you. Or you may be sitting in your cabin writing or

– thinking of me; I shall quietly sit down beside you and hold your dear hand. When will it really happen, Anselm? At present we have to be satisfied with being together in our thoughts, but knowing that we are is nice too; I wouldn't like to give it up. I have my own idea of your cabin, I wonder if it looks like this: when you come in the door, your desk is opposite on the left, at an angle in the corner, left of it is a little window to the ship and to the right of the desk one which looks straight onto the sea. Your bed is to the right of the door (as you come in) and there is a small table in the middle; the wash-stand is to the right of the little window that looks onto the sea. That's how I imagine it, which may of course be quite wrong, but that doesn't matter, because I've grown so fond of this picture of it, as I am with you so often in this cabin, as I am now. If you too have such lovely sunshine there, I'm sure you'll be quite sunburned, and then we will suit each other, as everyone looks at me in astonishment and asks which resort I have been to to get so brown and no one believes that the sun in Essen has done it. My 'inward' sun has certainly contributed to it. I can see before me the waxing moon as a narrow crescent; I wonder if you are watching it too? Tomorrow is Sunday. If only it would bring me post from you. But usually when you have reached a climax of impatience you are punished, and have to wait a little longer, but surely an answer must come soon. It has never been so long before, but probably just because I am longing for it so much.

There, Anselm, now I have at last sat beside you for a while and now I must leave you again in your cabin. Sleep well, my dear, best Anselm, and dream of your Maria.

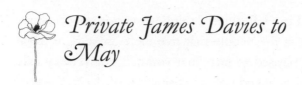

Private James Davies to May

James Davies enlisted in October 1917 and until the end of the war he wrote more than eighty letters to his sweetheart, May, back home in Accrington in Lancashire. From this letter, written from his training camp, we learn that they have already begun the common practice of exchanging love tokens and meeting the parents. And now, in another effort to feel closer, he sends her a button from his tunic.

14 NOV 1917

D coy
51st Grad Batt
Manchester Regiment
Campesdown
Great Yarmouth

Dear May,

I write these few lines in answer to your ever welcome letter dated the 12th and was pleased to hear that you had been to tea to our house and that you got on very well with them all which I expected would be the case although I am afraid you would not find it a mansion but it means a good deal to me I can tell you as I think we are not particular are we so long as the people that live there are allright. Dear May, I was pleased to hear that you had received my card and badge allright and I am enclosing one of the buttons off my tunic, it was jet black the other day all my buttons were as we went through the gas chamber, a chamber filled with the poison gas they use at the front of course we had our gas helmets on and the only effect it had on us was to turn everything we had on us that was metal jet black even the money in our pockets and am sorry to say that I forgot to take that ring off and it has changed the colour of it but it is coming round a little bit now the same as this button. Dear May, you say you wanted to speak to me last Thursday about something but I don't quite understand what you mean I am afraid it was a bit sharp the parting but never mind the war can't last for ever and it will be a good job when it is all over and we can come back to dear old Accrington again and you must not let that other matter bother your head perhaps you thought I was a bit quiet on the station but you know it is no easy job leaving home and so I hope you will excuse me as I really never thought of it until I got back so now I must close hoping that this finds you and all at home in the best of health so it leaves me and the boys at present I remain yours ever true

Jim xxxxxxxx

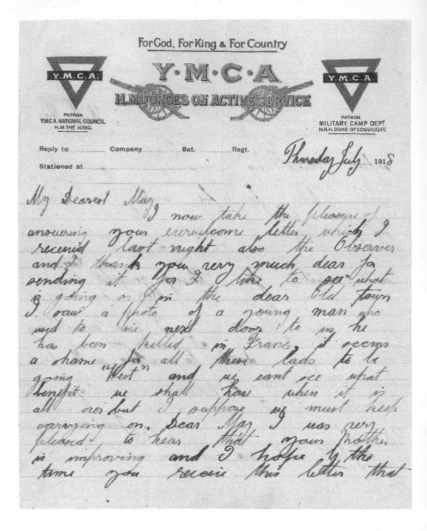

*Private James Davies wrote this letter to May on YMCA-
headed paper in 1918. The YMCA supported the troops
throughout the war, providing them with food and shelter
on the front line, in camps and railway stations.*

Private Guillaume Apollinaire to Madeleine Pagès

Guillaume Apollinaire was France's great poet of the First World War. He had enlisted in the army as soon as war broke out, and in January 1915, he met Madeleine Pagès, a young schoolteacher, on a train when he was returning from leave having visited his mistress. They exchanged addresses and a few months later began a correspondence. By August of that year, they were engaged and Apollinaire's letters then became increasingly erotic.

11 October 1915

My love, I had 2 letters from you today. I am very happy with them, you sound more like Poppaea and Phèdre now. I love you so much like this. Especially out here, where your precious sensuality is a consolation to me, the sole remedy for all my troubles. Please do mark this well, my love. You said yourself that we should strengthen the secret between us, so do strengthen it, and fear for nothing. Be naked before me – as far away as I am. Do not mention leave again for the time being. They have cancelled all leave in the forward zone all along the Front. Those on leave at present are therefore either from the depots or from the rear of the zone of operations. The infantry sometimes goes to the rear for rest periods, but we do not. Our group has never yet been sent back for rest. It is assumed that we have enough free time (and hence rest) where we are. Your meaningful look in Marseilles is admirably clear to me in memory, charged with all the voluptuousness that is part of you. You are very beautiful. I kiss your mouth through your hat veil, tearing it like a Veil of Isis and grasping the whole of that little traveller who is now my own beloved little wife and clasping her madly to me. Ah yes my love we shall know perfectly how to tell each other of our love and how to say it with our lips as well as our eyes.

It was charming, exquisite of you to tell me what you did after leaving me on the station platform at Marseilles and also the whole story of the amorous struggle that has been taking place within you since then. I love you. So we loved each other at very first sight. That is marvellous. I adore you.

My darling, I love this dear love story of ours and I take your whole mouth and kiss it, and then your breasts, so sensitive, whose tips harden at my kiss and strain towards me like your desire itself. I wrap my arms about you and hold you tight forever against my heart.

This is the time of day when the epeirids, cruciferous spiders, strew their gossamer all around. Looking at these white threads that the breeze tosses about and causes to shimmer in the light makes me think of you oh my adorable lily.

Today we were treated to the splendid sight of a homeward-bound squadron of 28 bombers intercepted by our fighter planes. The clash took place very high up, albeit not as high as our love, and the sky was speckled with thousands of white puffs of smoke from the explosions. A spectacle at once agonising and fascinating. Such a new kind of refinement! In the distance along the two fronts the vile priapic sausage-balloons maintained their defiantly immobile watch like maggots hatched in a rotting field of blue. It is perhaps these grubs that give birth to such graceful butterflies, the aeroplanes.

As for you, I adore you. I take you naked as a pearl and devour you with kisses all over from your feet to your head, so swoon from love, my darling love, I eat your mouth and your fine breasts which belong to me and which swollen with voluptuousness thrill me with endless delight.

Gui

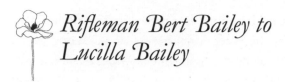

Rifleman Bert Bailey to Lucilla Bailey

Bert Bailey and Lucilla had married on 5 June 1915, on Bert's last leave, and through their letters, they tried to establish a married life of sorts. You can tell they haven't been married long: their letters don't have the relaxed intimacy so apparent in those between more established couples. But clearly, all Lucilla's love and concern for her new husband is expressed in the many home comforts she sends him in her parcels. And despite the circumstances, Bert still tries to maintain his role as protective husband and keeper of the household expenses.

But Bert and Lucilla weren't given the chance to conduct their marriage for real: a few hours after writing this letter, Bert was killed.

Wednesday, 27 October 1915

My Darling Wife,

Another night has passed and another morning come and I am still in the trenches and in good health. Although all day and night on Monday it rained steadily yet Tuesday (yesterday) morning broke fair and fine and we had a nice day except that underneath everything was mud and slosh. We were employed all the morning and afternoon in putting down boards along the trenches and have greatly improved it for walking. As I stopped to rest awhile I could not help being struck by the exceptional beauty of the moon as the clouds kept flitting past. The moon was nearly full, partially obscured by the thin fleecy clouds but these soon passed by and after a spell of clear shining the great black billows slowly closed in until it could only be seen shining dimly through a great rift in the clouds, then the whole closed up. The sky at that spot was absolutely black, but there was no rain, and although the great black ugly side was turned to me I knew the other side must be shimmering with the pure white light. Let us hope that this time of our lives is like that, a great dark cloud which passes away, so that afterwards the light is brighter than before.

Just a few words now about your last parcel. I don't often mention everything, but I do appreciate the rag you sent me, it is so very useful. The piece this week is lovely and I make a very shrewd guess that, when I am using it as a tablecloth, it was not always used for that purpose but once formed part of my lady's – 'Oh dear, oh dear, what am I saying' – nevertheless, it is grand to wrap my bread in and keep my food clean and nice. <u>Cigarettes – capital</u> but don't send any more until I ask you to. <u>Toffee, condensed milk, candles, rice and potted meat:</u> the toffee, milk, rice and one candle have all gone. Potted meat for tea today, candle tonight if necessary. The Oxo cubes will be very nice to augment my soup with no doubt. Don't send me any more Oxo or Bovril until I ask you to, darling, will you. The little pat of butter is always welcome, and the bread dodge I think is an improvement on buying expensive cakes. Of course a little home-made cake is nice, but I was never a lover of cake. Please discontinue sending tea, sugar and salt for a bit, Darling, as I have plenty. Don't think I am trying to economize and stint myself because it is not that, and it all helps us, dear, doesn't it?

Now my little Darling, you must be patient with me won't you and don't get cross because I have been having a lot to say about the parcels. You are a pet to send them and you know you asked me to guide you as to what I most required, didn't you?

The pastry of your own make was absolutely A1, and a perfect success – and she's the little girl who said, 'Oh, I can only cook a plain dinner.' One great thing is off my mind and that is that I need never fear for my life in the future when you send me or make me pastry!

The weather has remained fine all the afternoon and let's hope it will be fine tonight. A cold night's bad, but a wet cold night is worse. You must not worry about me, Darling, because I am just as able to look after myself as the other chaps. So, dearest little one, just keep cheerful and enjoy yourself all you can, and wrap up now the cold is here. If you require new clothes in the way of an overcoat or mac or gloves or anything for the winter, don't let yourself go short will you? Just take it from the cash and note it in the book as I told you, so that we can see how the cash is made up for the sake of keeping proper accounts. I'm afraid I twaddle a lot but never mind.

I remain

ever your own devoted

Bert

Edward Marcellus to Goldie Marcellus

Edward Marcellus was an American clerk stationed in the German camps taken over by the Allies at the end of the war. He and his wife Goldie had an unusual letter-writing system: Goldie would send him her affectionate, chatty, handwritten letters, and Edward would type brief, often humorous, remarks on her letter and send them back. There is no clue as to why they did this. Maybe it was to save paper, or perhaps it was just his way of keeping the situation light and free from strain.

There is no date on this letter, but it was probably written some time in 1919. Edward's replies are in bold.

Dear Husband,

This is a Sat. afternoon and I have the work all done and washing on the line. **Smart girl** I do not know what they would do without me I must say. I am sure very tired. You see Mamma is sick at Proctor Hospital & Dad away and Gladys is not real strong & Hila will not work too hard **No** for fear she might spoil her buty beauty. **Yes, Booty is right.**

Mother is getting along fine just now. **That's good.**

Excuse this writing for my arm is so tired. When I was home I did not know what work was. **I didn't think so.** I received a letter from Pearl. **Why don't she write to me?** She is not well at all poor girl. I think she will never get strong now. She says that her husband comes home at night and does up all of the housework. **Very nice of him.** It is hard on him, but it sure is nice that he is so willing to do it. Your mother goes over and does the washing & ironing & the baking. **and talking.** So you see that she must be a very weak woman. **Yes, you are right.** One should be so happy if they have good health.

I took your picture to church with me. (You see I must have you with me that is all.) **That is a catastrophe.**

Everyone thought you sure was a fine **fat** looking young man. Our preacher's wife, a most lovely lady, said, 'your husband sure is nice looking' and the preacher said, 'not only he, but he is the possessor of a nice looking young wife.' I will look more pretty when you get home, **dots gut** for I will be far more happy. I want to keep myself looking well for you and you alone. We both must keep our health at any cost, for health and looks go well together. I hope and pray you can come home soon.

Your picture stands right in front of me this very moment. **Why don't you send me some of yours? I have worn yours out already.** I can hardly believe it is you. The only part that looks natural is your eyes. **And what about them?** I just have to kiss that sweet fat face every time I look at your picture. Well I must stop a bragging on for you might run away with some pretty girl over there. Ha. Ha. **There isn't any.**

So some of the men in your Co. go with girls. **No, not girls, fraulines.** Well dear Ed, I expect there is much more of 'not being loyal' by the girls over here. Yes, I know all about them. I just read in the paper where a returned soldier came back only to find the one he had been true to in love with another man, so he killed her. **Yes, you'll find the members of the A.E.F. are not afraid to kill.** I do not believe in killing but she really got what she deserved I must say. I guess one side is as bad as the other.

Do not even let Herb know this, but I prayed for Gladys C. not to give him up & marry some other man too sickly to fight for his own country. Several weeks ago she came to me on her way home from work, her eyes filled with tears and said, 'Goldie, oh help me out, you are a married girl and one of my dearest friends.' **I really am not surprised at this but do not tell her I said so.** I won her on the point that she did not know men at all, if she would turn untrue to Herb he being such a strong man, would just go all to pieces **Yes, I believe he would** and just throw his life away. Well she went home and thought it over and now 'all is well' and Herb is alone shining in Gladys's sky. **Good, you're a missionary too.** Oh, I have read some of Herb's letters and Ed his future entirely rests with that girl. I sure am happy over the outcome.

Oh see it is mail time and I do want to get this in the box by 4.30. So I will have to close. (I could write to you by the hrs.)

Take good care of yourself and I will do the same. So By By my dear hubby, I enclose all love for you

From your loving wife

Goldie

Ed

III. SEPARATION AND LONGING

A soldier's home leave was a rarity, for many an impossibility, and relationships were severely tried and tested by such long periods apart. Many rose to the challenge but others were driven to the depths of despair. Some of the most beautiful and heartfelt letters were written during times of separation when, in calm reflection, love rose to the surface and was captured in words.

Abschied des Kriegers.

1. Das Vaterland ruft
uns hinaus,
Hinaus zum scharfen
Streit,
Für Weib und Kind,
für Hof und Haus
Sind wir zum Kampf
bereit.

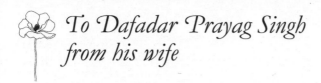

To Dafadar Prayag Singh from his wife

Over one million soldiers of the British Indian Army fought in the Great War, and many served for the entire duration. It would have been difficult for an Indian couple to stay regularly in touch by letter and even more impossible to be granted leave. Dafadar Prayag Singh's wife wrote to him in dramatic terms about the depths of her despair.

Moradabad
Uttar Pradesh

20 February 1917

My husband,

My heart feels that it could not sustain separation from you for a single minute; but it is now three years since I was last blessed with your presence – what then must my heart suffer! I am wandering alone in the wilderness of this world. I cannot realize when it was that I last looked on your face, and I would thankfully give my life as an offering to anyone who would bring me into your presence once more. What words of yours, my dear, need I recall to mind, when my very veins are full of love for you! And how can I enjoy any degree of happiness in separation from you! Therefore I make this one request, that you should send for me, or write and tell me to come to you. But tell me precisely the place you are in, so that I may not fail to find it. You write to me about money, but what care I for money. I need you alone! I am in need of nothing else, and I do not hanker after riches. I am my lord's handmaid, and would count it happiness even to starve in my lord's presence. May God speedily bring the day when I, the grief-laden one, gazing in the glory of your countenance, will renew my life.

Your wife

A conscientious objector to his wife

This Scottish conscientious objector had been in prison in Scotland for nearly three years. In the few letters that have been preserved, he is mostly concerned with the difficulties his wife faces with accommodation: when landlords find out she is married to a 'conchie' she is asked to leave. Here, for a change, he gives free rein to his literary and sensual imagination.

There is no date on this letter but it was probably written in 1919. 'My heart is like a singing bird,' he says in another letter later that year as he learns of his impending release.

My sweet mistress,

I wonder whether in the far-off South, after so long a separation – nearly three years – you think of your absent lover, whether you miss him, whether your spirit and your flesh cry out for him, whether you ever strive to picture and to taste what our reunion will mean and be.

In these days, oh, so very often since I woke up last June, I have wanted you, wanted you as I never wanted you before. I have lain awake night after night, calling 'Dearest, Dearest', until I have had to cover my pillow with passionate kisses, since your luscious lips and smooth shoulders and soft breasts were denied me. I have pretended that the fingers stroking my body and breasts, plucking my nipples, were yours; but nothing I could do could fill my arms, be your body and breasts and limbs as they used to press to mine, could give me my sweet, loving, ardent, tender mistress.

Did you ever want me like that? Psyche has been so reticent. But I do not reproach her for her silence, a silence not of apathy or indifference, a silence preserved solely to dam back that flood of warm, passionate feeling which she will pour forth for her lover till its waves bear him to the River of Delight, to the fathomless Sea of Love, whose islands are Cytherea, and whose airs are zephyrs of intoxicating fragrance and music.

How gracious a personality has my mistress! Merely to recite the phases of her sweet revealing is to summon from the past a succession of sweethearts, all the famous lovers of myth and ballad enfolded in one warm, palpitating, lovely form of modern days. The struggling Diana under the trees at Hendon, who could not bear that her lover should kiss even the nape of her neck; the weeping Cassandra of Wayland Common; the quiet, trustful Miranda of Milton Mill, whose dreams took on warmer colours under her lover's caresses; the smiling Shulamite who pleaded for her left breast's little sister; the froward pagan of Fin Glen who would not bathe but relenting bade her lover possess her from her lips to her waist; the confident guide of Dunmore, who rewarded the seeker at 55; the tender sweetheart of October and of Christmas; the wedded maid of Dumfries; the imperious Valkyrie of Inverkip, whose ardours roused even her sluggish steed to a breathless gallop; the jesting Venus of Nether Raith; the bonniest, tenderest, warmest, dearest of all mistresses.

I shall post this letter at once.

All love

A

Lieutenant Roland Leighton to Vera Brittain

The correspondence between Roland Leighton and Vera Brittain is one of the most famous of the Great War. Their letters are extremely eloquent (Roland was a poet, Vera an author in embryo who went on to write the memoir Testament of Youth*) but they have a natural quality and don't strive to be literary.*

Roland's feelings in this short letter are beautifully expressed. It was written just as he returned to France after a few days' leave, during which he and Vera became engaged.

In Billets
France
26 August 1915, 2.30 p.m.

I got back here at about 11.30 a.m. this morning after a rather tiring journey by train and motor. I found your long letter waiting for me. It was so strange in a way to read something that you had written before you saw me and when my coming back at all was only problematical. And now it seems to count for so little that I did come back after all, so little that I saw and talked with what was no longer a dream but a reality, and found in My Lady of Letters a flesh and blood princess. Did we dream it after all, dearest? No; for if we had it would not have hurt so much. I am feeling very weary and very very triste – rather like (as is said of Lyndall) 'a child whom a long day's play has saddened'. And it is all so unreal – even the moon and the sea last night. All is unreal but the memory and the pain and the insatiable longing for Something which one has loved.

There is sunshine on the trees in the garden and a bird is singing behind the hedge. I feel as if someone had uprooted my heart to see how it was growing.

Roland Leighton was killed in December 1915. His grave is regularly strewn with violets in remembrance of this poem he wrote for Vera.

Violets

Violets from Plug Street Wood
Sweet, I send you oversea.
(It is strange they should be blue,
Blue when his soaked blood was red;
For they grew around his head:
It is strange they should be blue.)
Violets from Plug Street Wood
Think what they have meant to me –
Life and Hope and Love and You.
(And you did not see them grow
Where his mangled body lay,
Hiding horror from the day.
Sweetest, it was better so.)
Violets from oversea,
To your dear, far, forgetting land:
These I send in memory,
Knowing You will understand.

Violets — April 1915

Violets from Plug Street Wood,
Sweet, I send you oversea.
(It is strange they should be blue,
Blue, when his soaked blood was red,
For they grew around his head;
It is strange they should be blue.)
Violets from Plug Street Wood
Think what they have meant to me —
Life and Hope and Love and You
(And you did not see them grow
Where his mangled body lay,
Hiding horror from the day;
Sweetest, it was better so.)

Violets from oversea,
To your dear, far, forgetting land
These I send in memory,
Knowing You will understand.

R.A.L.

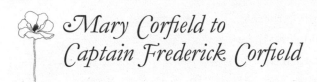

Mary Corfield to
Captain Frederick Corfield

This marriage was severely tested by the war. Frederick Corfield served the entire duration of the conflict and his almost permanent absence left his wife in a deep depression, which was always particularly acute after a leave. In this letter, she captures perfectly the bittersweet nature of these brief reunions.

Draycott Place
Kensington

Saturday 6.30 pm
March 17 1917

My Own Darling,

Only just a few lines while Evelyn is out, as I've got the grumps <u>badly</u> & am missing you frightfully – I feel I said goodbye to you simply <u>horribly</u> & didn't say anything I wanted to, but Darling I should have broken down completely & as I knew that was the last thing either of us wanted I thought it best to make off with a terribly heavy heart which felt just like breaking & I just didn't care a bit what anyone thought of me as I walked along the Embankment to Scotland Yard, just longing that I could be alone somewhere.

Oh Darling these partings are <u>awful</u> & yet without them, there couldn't be the meetings – what wouldn't I have given I wonder to have been you going back this afternoon to all your work and interests, for I don't think you can have time to feel the awful restlessness that I feel & oh such a heartache. But I suppose it's easy enough to say this when we can have no idea of all the horrors & discomforts – & if <u>only</u> all is going to be well by the end of the year, then we can & must 'carry on' cheerfully. But it's mighty hard at times & there is always the thought of this 'great show' hanging over ones' heads.

Oh these leaves they are <u>very</u> lovely but my word they are unsettling. I badly want something to buck me up for dinner tonight!!!

Goodnight you Darling Thing. I shall feel better after a good old howl when I get to bed tonight & hope to continue more cheerfully tomorrow – but it's so hard to be cheerful the first night. I wonder if the old man is missing 'her' as much as she is 'him'?–

God bless you my Darling & every bit of good luck to you. Thank you ever so much Darling for the lovely time you gave me –

Ever such a hug

Your devoted & very sad

Missus

Marthe Gylbert to an unknown Australian soldier

Marthe Gylbert had been evacuated with her family from Armentières in summer 1917, when the village was being heavily bombarded by the Germans, to St-Sulpice-les-Feuilles in southern France. A year later she wrote this letter to her Australian sweetheart, whom she had met in Armentières. She decorated it carefully and elaborately, perhaps to compensate for the inadequacy of the English and the shortness of the letter, which was probably written on Marthe's behalf.

Saint Sulpice les Feuilles
25 August 1918

My Darling Little Sweetheart,

Just few lines hoping that my letter find you in the best of Health. I am very well myself at present and my family the same.

Well Lovey, you see I am faithfully thinking of you not too one else only to you. You know I love you very well my Little Husband. I am never love any body else. if you get killed I stay every time with my little Baby. if you give me one. I hope to see you very soon. Darling I Dream about you last night I see you married with one else.

So will close now with the best Remembrance from all my family and me.

Best Love and Kisses XXX from your ever Loving Little Sweetheart. Wife to be very soon.

Marthe Gylbert

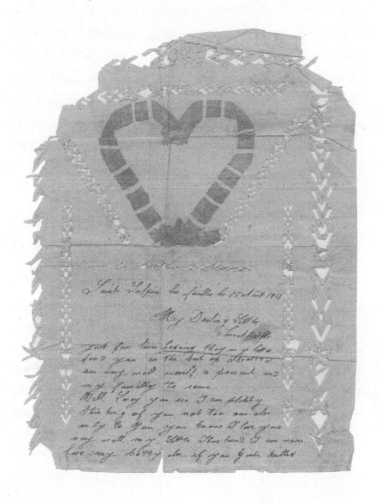

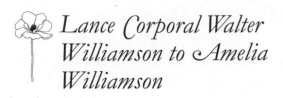

Lance Corporal Walter Williamson to ᴇAmelia Williamson

Walter Williamson was twenty-eight years old when he went to war with the 6th Battalion Cheshire Regiment, leaving behind his wife Amelia and two-year-old son 'Little Jimmy'. He had been in France for nearly two years when he wrote this beautiful letter, full of longing.

21 May 1918 – Tuesday 5 a.m.

Dear little sweetheart,

I had to be up at 4 this morning to get a runner off on a long trip, and as it is quite daylight I don't feel like getting to bed again. It is going to be such a glorious day again. I have such a glorious view from the window here, the mist is just rising, and a great filmy red sun is just peeping over a ridge right away in front. The grass is all shiny wet and glinting like myriads of wee diamonds, and diamond cobwebs in the bushes. The birds are all getting up and surely there must be heaps of little fluffy balls of babies in the nests as the chittering and chattering going on is immense. The old cock here has just been having a vocal argument with some old rooster further up the village, but has subsided and decided he will have another nod. Oh! and the smell with the blossoms and lilac (we have some lilac). One can hardly imagine there is a ghastly war on and that a lot of poor chaps are coughing out lyddite fumes and such like stinks after the usual morning hate has been hurled across.

Yours was a dear little letter yesterday. I know it must be hard for you, little woman, a man's feelings anytime, though perhaps rougher, are never, and never can be as keen as a woman's. I am not wanting you like I do sometimes in the heat of the day, or the heavy sensuousness of the close of a hot day. As I went through the gardens a few minutes since, a little leaf with the dew on just drew itself across my lips, oh so cool and sweet, just like your lips in your quiet moods. Just like you sitting up in bed early one morning, shaking your hair back and giving me one of those brushing kisses and saying 'Oh lad what a glorious morning it is.' This morning is just the sort of morning that you would say 'Just let us have a look down the garden before we have breakfast' and argue that your slippers were quite waterproof when they were not.

Reveille is just blowing now and I must rattle Len out of it. He can see no beauty in an early morning.

Just eight little kisses, one for your hair, one for each dear eye, one for the top of your nose, one for each cheek, one on the chin, and as it is rather early and you may not be quite dressed, one for each of your sweet little breasts, from your loving husband Walter

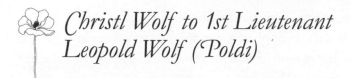

Christl Wolf to 1st Lieutenant Leopold Wolf ('Poldi)

The Wolfs were a young Viennese couple who, like the Wightmans on pages 170–2, conducted their courtship, marriage and arrival of their first child through the entire duration of the war. Apart from the occasional home leave, these landmark events had to be experienced through their letters, and Christl referred to their marriage as 'a short beautiful dream'. She wrote this letter to Leopold just a few weeks after the birth of their daughter and on learning that his request for a transfer nearer home had been denied. Her sadness at their lost youthful happiness is very affecting.

Vienna 11 May 1918.

Dearest Poldi!

What I guessed and feared for so long has now become reality, I wrote to you about it in my last letter before I knew for sure. I have no words for such disappointment, what good would it do? Whether I curse or complain, it changes nothing, I go on brooding all day about why things had to be this way. All our lovely hopes destroyed, for God knows how long, and this dreadful loneliness, it causes me so much suffering, however much I might try to pull myself together, for the sake of our little girl, I find it terribly hard. Often

I feel so desolate that I would like to bury myself away. I barely dare to hope that you will come back even for a few days, because in that case you would have been here for ages already. Your letters, so rare of late, cannot improve my mood. You will not be much better of course, but you are in the middle of your work, which is why you get the chance to write so rarely, and your thoughts are so much more distracted than mine, as I sit here waiting in vain day after day, having set everything up, and thinking with every single touch, that's for my Poldi, or you'll like that, every time I look at my child I imagine you being able to see her as I do. It's a time that's lost for ever. But dearest Poldi let me conclude now, I'm not in the mood right now to write a letter, and I only did it because you'll have to wait so long anyway. I've had nothing for 3 days again. Nothing surprises me any more. Our little girl is well, thank God.

She gets cuter and livelier every day, a sign that she feels very well.

Big hugs and deep kisses from your lonely desperate Wifey

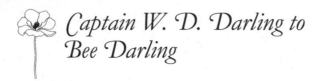

Captain W. D. Darling to Bee Darling

Douglas and Bee Darling's courtship was a long one by war standards. He wrote to her regularly, and in his very loving letters he would say over and over again how much he missed her. Finally they married, but instead of it sating his desire for her, it made the agony of his longing much more acute.

France

22 Jan 1918

Dear Love,

No mail today. It has been a quiet day; little work, and lovely frosty weather. I have been playing bridge in the mess and it is so cold that I am chilled through – so I am sitting over the fire to write you a few lines before I go to bed.

Dear heart, I want you so. I am tired of so much masculine companionship, and I long to have my own little woman to talk to every day. Before I met you I used to love the freedom and camaraderie of camp life – but now I hate it all, and long for you.

Ah, my own darling, I hope I will be with you soon. You are so sweet and loving and lovely – I long to pet and cuddle you and admire you. For the second time I am beginning to believe that our marriage is only a lovely dream; when we are separated so much, it is hard to believe that all those lovely honeymoon nights really happened! I long for our third honeymoon – I want to play with you, fondle you, and then seduce you – and then to admire you and hug and fondle you again – and then when you are quite shivery, to warm you under the bedclothes until you are ready for more fondling! Ah, my own love, I am aching to have you in my arms again. All my heart is yours, and I pray for you always. God bless you.

    Your ever loving

        Douglas

Private Marcel Rivier to Louise Rivier

Marcel Rivier was a twenty-one-year-old Algerian soldier and he had never had a sweetheart. He began a war diary, starting on the first day of mobilization and ending on the day of his death on 4 November 1914, and in it he poured out his longing for love. But because the only female touch he had known was his mother's, all his yearnings were wrapped up in her, as if he couldn't make the leap from maternal to sensual love. This poem was addressed to his mother.

Tender Evening

Oh! This evening I tremble with tenderness
I think of you as I find myself alone and feel myself far away,
Far from all that my fond heart craves so badly
As it falters between hope and sadness

Like a wounded bird, my weary heart – so easily scarred –
Longs for the safest of nests, a small corner
Where peacefully, in the sweetness of devoted care
Pain could melt hazily into weakness

It hungers for words that are quietly intimate, honeyed and slow
The kind of words that rise up from the bottom of the soul
Falling from my lips in small plaintive blows

And I dream of fingers that are light, deft and white
Laid cool and quivering on my eyes
If not a mother's fingers, then at least a woman's fingers
Banishing the vision of grisly memories

Your Marcel
October 1914

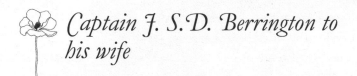

Captain J. S. D. Berrington to his wife

Captain Berrington, who commanded a Royal Flying Corps Kite Balloon Section in France, wrote to his wife from hospital whilst recovering from shellshock. He's so ill he can barely write and his handwriting is strange and unsteady, but in just a couple of paragraphs he manages to convey, and without self-pity, how much he desperately needs his wife's comfort.

No 8 General Hospital

Rouen

7 June 1916

Little thing,

I wonder if you have had all my letters – I've written every day since the shell burst – at first I thought I should be alright, but then the usual things came along – headache, loss of memory & general breakup – so I had to go to hospital & was 5 days in the first – one day in the clearing hospital – & now here at the Base – & today rather cheap. How I envy the men who have gone home today – & wish I was on my way to you. But I have always thought of you & your birthday present, my Darling – & the knowledge that you are really mine – it makes things better – much – but I do long for you – & a green tree – & the murmur of a river – taken in their order, the three best things on earth to me.

In my ward there are 16 beds – a long low wood-walled tin-roofed place – sometimes the noise is a trouble – but usually I am comfy – with 2 extra blankets & a hot water bottle & for once I am glad enough to be in bed. Some are sent home to convalesce – some do it in France. I pray for home. Au revoir, my Darling Wife.

Your own J

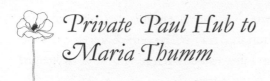

Private Paul Hub to Maria Thumm

Paul Hub and Maria became engaged two days before Paul departed for army training in August 1914. When he writes to Maria, he is quite candid about the dangerous conditions and his near-misses; he even sends her farewell letters on the eve of battle, so perhaps it is no wonder that she is ever anxious.

26 April 1917

Darling,

Again your letters are full of fear and anxiety. You don't realize how well we are doing right now. You write about blood, death and horrific battles. But the fighting isn't like that. We are several kilometres behind the Front and are not thinking of death and the horrors of war. Why do you keep going on about it? If fighting is going on somewhere on the Western Front, it doesn't necessarily mean we are in the thick of it. You see, dearest, your non-stop fretting is depressing me. Here I am, enjoying some peace in my nice lodgings full of the joys of spring and there you are at home worrying. Darling, I understand you and your worries all too well. But you shouldn't read so much into what they write in the papers. When you were off skiing, I thought of you happily going up and down the slopes. If you read about a battle in the newspaper, tell yourself I am not there. Ninety-nine times out of one hundred you will be right. So don't grumble unnecessarily. You only make me nervous. And it makes me admire my sorely tested parents.

Greetings from your true love,

Paul

2nd Lieutenant Clifford Vincent
to Iris Dutton

Schoolteacher Clifford Vincent was engaged to Iris Dutton when he enlisted with the Lancashire Hussars. In this letter, he goes to great lengths to reassure and comfort her about the situation they find themselves in. His tone is so measured and rational that you long for him to stop being the schoolteacher and start being the lover – and then he delivers his wonderful last line.

France
1st Sept 1917

My darling sweetheart,

I was very sorry not to have written to you yesterday, but I will do my best to make up for it. I was very glad to receive your dear letter just now. It did me very much good indeed. Also I was very much entertained to read Dad's letter to you. In it he says that he advised us (his sons) not to take extra risks, in our search for decorations. Now I have been fortunate enough to win a decoration and it may seem to you that I have disregarded his advice. No, carissima, I did not. I went into an attack with orders to do certain things. I did them as well as I could, and the award came along. No, my darling, I'm not cowardly, but I'm taking no extra risks. There's <u>you</u> and <u>I want to come back to you</u>, as soon as ever

I can. So please don't worry. There is only one thing you can do and that you always do. You pray for me. Your prayers, like sweet pleading spirits, ascend to the Father and win for me his gracious care and protection. So fiancée de moi, pray on.

I, returning to look at your letter, notice that it is rather sad. What is the matter, dear girl? I think I know what it is. You are lonely and loneliness ever breeds sadness. You are minus a great deal of the love that is so necessary to a spirit such as yours. But although it is not there in the flesh, there is always the love of Him whose love is perfection. So, cheer up, sweetheart, for soon will be restored to you all the love that should be around you. Do you know I think it is my fault that you were deceived about my coming home. I gave you too much hope. I am really very sorry, dearest heart, but you must always remember this fact that you can never depend upon anything concerning army promises because things are altered many times in one day. That is what we told you. So please don't reckon on seeing me until you receive my telegram from London. Then you will be happy and gay again and what a good time we will have.

Iris, I am a bunch of longing dissolved in a sea of happiness in your love.

Yours forever,

Cliff

Amy Handley to Private John George Clifton (Jack)

Amy Handley and Jack Clifton had known each other since 1913. Amy was a nursemaid in a big house, a small boy was her charge. Her letters to Jack are all written in the same breathless, fractured style, as if she is losing her mind with the need for him.

This is the last letter she wrote. It is undated because the first page is missing, but it was sent some time after 21 July 1918. Jack was killed in action on 21 August 1918.

[Lavendon, Olney, Bucks]

Jack – my own – my only love – how I look for your next letter – How much longer shall I have to wait? Dearheart, I want you – My life – Jack – how changed it is when you are by my side – what different air I seem to breathe into my lungs–! Jack – Jack – Oh! hasten the day – the moment when I shall be by his side again – Jack – my Jack – my same, same heartmate – Goodnight my love – God bless you my own. Tuesday Jickie Jock – my own & how today? How you would have smiled if you could have met me up the road today – Yes! you would then – To have seen me pushing David in his pram to Brayfield all on my own – Jack, if only – but then how can I say, how can I express all that is in my heart – ? Does my Jack know – ? My love, my own, at such moments,

Jack, when my love has looked, has seen into the very depths of my soul – My Jack – My, 'Our' sacred love – when my very soul has been revealed to him – Jack – you know – How it grows & grows – My heart – Surely it will burst – Jack – Jack – I want you – Oh! let me feel you crushing my very life into yours – Jack – Jack – I live for you – always, always my own

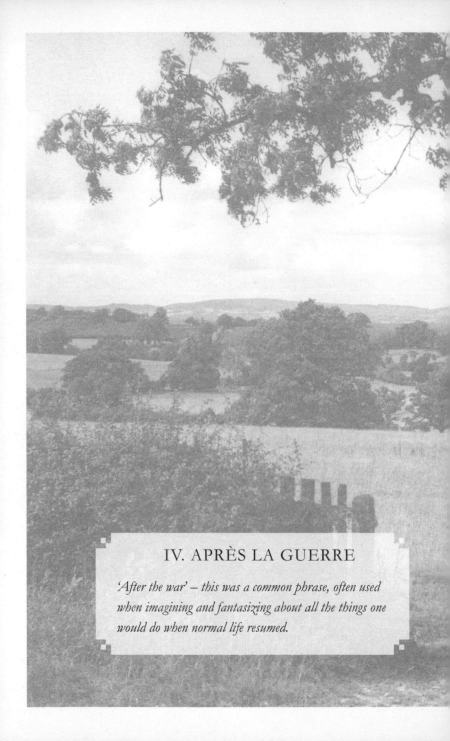

IV. APRÈS LA GUERRE

'After the war' – this was a common phrase, often used when imagining and fantasizing about all the things one would do when normal life resumed.

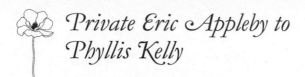

Private Eric Appleby to
Phyllis Kelly

Eric Appleby was from Liverpool. He enlisted in 1914 and was sent to Athlone in Ireland for training. There he met local girl Phyllis Kelly at a dance. Over the next two years, as their romance deepened, they exchanged over two hundred letters. Eric was very dependent on Phyllis's letters, and writing to her was fundamental to his wellbeing. In some, he would recount at great length every detail of their last meeting, but here, he is looking forwards rather than backwards.

Tuesday 17 October 1916

My darling

Oh! I got the very dearest lovely letter from you yesterday. The one about the weekend we would have on our own in your house, and what we would do with it. Really, lady mine, I can forget all about this beastliness while I read this letter, and how I long to be able to do everything just as you say we would have done. I'm afraid, though, I would have been turned out of the kitchen for trying to make love, because the whole letter makes me just ache and ache with love for my Lady.

I have never eaten a flapjack, as far as I know. Don't they consist of flour, baking powder, suet or butter and water, or something of that kind? However, I know they would be luscious as long as you made them. I feel just as though I want to dance and dance round all over the place, and I'm sure I would pick you up (much against your wishes) and whisk you from the kitchen. Yes, perhaps I would sit and sulk when you teased me because I wanted loving very badly, but oh! sweetheart, I can just imagine how very wonderfully dear you would be when you melted and came to me.

And now for our evening. Well, first we would get ready for dinner, and you would put on – what? – that sweet grey dress with the sticky-up Elizabethan collar. Then we'd have a nice dinner all to ourselves, and afterwards, when everything was cleared away and the curtains drawn and the chairs close to the fire, then we'd put out the lamp and make a good blaze. You'd kneel down and poke away at the fire till it blazed up. Then you would perhaps take your knitting, while I would gaze into the fire and think of how wonderful it was in 'heaven on earth' away from all this horribleness. Then you would have got tired of sitting curled up, and I would put my arms around you and lift you towards me. Then I would draw your head back ever so gently until you looked full up into my face as I bent down. Then a wonderful love quiver would run through me and I would bend down further and kiss you full on the lips. I can almost see those dear hands holding the knitting drop to your lap when I took your head in my hands, and I can feel the wonderful thrill of real love go through me as my lips touch yours. The minutes would slip away and the hours would fly, and still we would forget the time. What would it matter; we could stay where we were because then our world could go on without us having to think of going to bed. Perhaps we could go to bed, though, very, very late, and we would give each other a final goodnight kiss. Then we'd creep off to our rooms and dream lovely, happy dreams, to be told the next day.

Now, sweetheart, I must turn in; it's 10.30 and I've got to do night-firing at 1.15. Every atom of my love to you, dear one forever,

Your Englishman

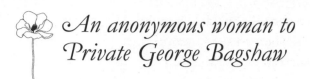

An anonymous woman to Private George Bagshaw

This is a partial letter which was forwarded to George Bagshaw's family by his regiment. We have no idea who the sender is, nor are there any clues as to why this couple's relationship has been so flimsy and uncommunicative. However, a note in the archive file reports that he died of wounds, 17 May 1918, nearly a year before she sends this letter. She has left it far too late. And it seems fitting somehow, that just as she begins to encourage him to return, to imagine the possibility, the letter ends and there is no more.

April 22nd 1919

Dear George,

Just a few lines hoping you are in the best of health as it leaves me at present, and all at home the same. Dear George, I have received no letter from you yet, I know you haven't much time, but I thought I should have had one by now. It is a fortnight I began to think George that you had got tired of me, but when I read your mother's letter, I know you still remember me. Dear George, I don't think you will know that Ernest has got wounded, he is in hospital at the Base. Well dear, you don't know how it feels when I don't get a letter from you, they talk about it breaking your heart, but it has nearly broke mine. I should have written a few letters but I didn't know where to send them to, it seems better when you know you can write. Well dear Mr Hughes was asking about you the other day, and the Sister asked me to go to the Mission as she is leaving, and so I went on Sunday, it seemed like old times, but they are not the same faces that I used to see. Dear George you trust in God, and perhaps with a bit of luck you will come back, we shall keep ourselves up, and then see what. Dear George, choose how you come back, you will find

Agnes Miller to Olaf Stapledon

Agnes Miller and Olaf Stapledon were cousins: Agnes was Australian, Olaf was English. They had met only a handful of times, when Agnes and her family had been visiting their English relatives, but Agnes and Olaf were drawn to each other and since 1913, they had conducted a long-distance relationship by letter. In 1915, Olaf joined the Friends' Ambulance Unit, and their almost daily letter-writing continued. In this letter, Agnes imagines a picnic they'll have together when the war is over, but despite the happy prospect she can't help worrying that after such a long time apart, Olaf might be disappointed with her.

Egremont, Mosman, Sydney, Australia
21 April 1918

My Olaf

There is only a strip of yellow sand between the lagoon & the sea & it looks like a gold bar on a field of blue, for you have to come to the beginning of the reef itself. Shall we have our lunch here among the sand hills – or shall we go out to the end first? It depends whether we feel hungry. Do you? 'Yes, starving.' So let's boil the billy for tea & spread our little feast here in the shade. I wonder what we shall talk about. I shall never be able to believe it is really you – you! Olaf of the letters. Olaf of the waiting – my Olaf – my lover! Will your eyes be always watching me? & when they have looked at all the beautiful hills & trees & the sea & the sky will they come back & rest on me? Oh I shall be happy but I shall be afraid too of what those eyes see in me. They will expect to find more than is there, & they may find, too, ugly things which they did not expect – but I shall not try & hide, & I shall not be really afraid because I know they will love me in spite of everything. I have been told I stare even at ordinary people I am interested in. What will be your fate? I promise not to 'stare' – I shall just open my eyes very wide & take you all into my heart. Oh my dear, my darling! Just think of it! And after lunch we'll lie & laze in the sun – perhaps we'll read a book – I'll read & you can smoke your old pipe (do you smoke nowadays?) or perhaps we'll just talk or just lie & then we'll hide our belongings in the bushes & set off up the springy grass headland towards the sea.

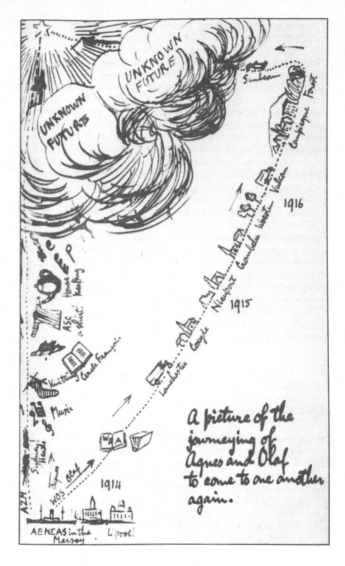

Olaf's depiction of his separation from Agnes and their imagined reunion, drawn on the back of a photograph and sent to Agnes in 1916.

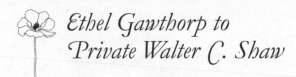

Ethel Gawthorp to
Private Walter C. Shaw

*Ethel Gawthorp and Walter Shaw had known each other since
1908 and probably met at their local church in Leeds. They were
engaged to be married. Ethel's* après la guerre *letter is very
touching. She has no grand plans, no extravagant fantasies about
what shape their life will take when he returns – just to be by
his side when he's welcomed back at church and to walk an old
familiar walk with him would be paradise enough. But on the
very same day Ethel wrote this letter, Walter was killed in the
Battle of the Somme.*

Meanwood Road
Leeds

Sat 1-7-16

Dearest Walter,

Thanks ever so much for your most encouraging letter.
'A few more week-ends & perhaps this business will be over.'
Oh that sentence was read and re-read. It was a grand letter,
dearie. Your trust in God is fine. I thanked God for having
given me such a good man. Oh bless you, I guess you will
appreciate a Sunday at home. Only to think of having you

next to me at Chapel, well laddie I'm sure of this, that I shall worship better. Of course I know that anyone's presence should not make any difference to our worshipping God but it takes a very saintly person to concentrate one's whole attention at a time like this. Then you say you will have tea in the basement. Now just fancy that. Why did you not say you would have it in 'la salle à manger'. Well I guess the basement will appear as a Paradise compared to your billets.

Oh what a grand reunion we shall have at the S. School when you all come home. My word the school will look full & how we shall talk. I wish someone had a camera & could just snap us. You would see hand-shaking & heads nodding, getting hold of your arm if your hands were full. I'm thinking that I shall begrudge anyone taking possession of you. But then you'll be able to save a lot of room for your girlie by your side, won't you, love? Oh won't it be grand when we meet again.

My word, I guess you have had a real bombardment and no mistake. It has gone on now for a week and as far as I read it looks like continuing. I pray that God will continue to watch over you & bring you safely through. I'm sure as Mrs Wood said this morning we must keep on praying and praying & never cease. That's just what we are doing, pet, night & day. If I wake in the night my thoughts go up to God for you. You are never out of my thoughts night & day. There! I must stop talking about the future. I sometimes wonder what we shall do when you come back again dear. Last week Bert Lee was saying oh when Walter comes back we shall never see you, or perhaps I shall come in & you'll say, well, I can go for a walk but I must be back at 7.30 or 8 because Walter is coming. I said, Oh, we'll wait and see, he might want to drill one or two nights per week & then I laughed.

Won't it be grand when you are walking up the road & then we walk over Sugar Well Hill & down that lane where we met on Sept 7th 1908. I think that is the right year. Well we have had a fairly rough passage but bless you there's a reward at the end & after all this is over we shall be able to say that Christ went with us all the way & he will continue to do so if we will only trust Him. You don't know how I'm longing to see you but there! your longing is just as great, I know, but keep smiling & put a cheerful courage on.

Now dear, no more at present. Good night and God bless you, my own brave darling & may you be kept under the shadow of the Almighty & may his choicest blessing rest upon you.

With best love
Ethel
Xxxxx

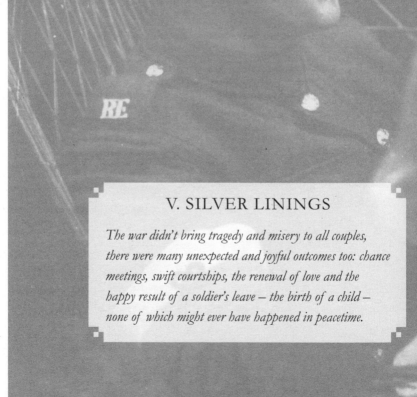

V. SILVER LININGS

*The war didn't bring tragedy and misery to all couples,
there were many unexpected and joyful outcomes too: chance
meetings, swift courtships, the renewal of love and the
happy result of a soldier's leave — the birth of a child —
none of which might ever have happened in peacetime.*

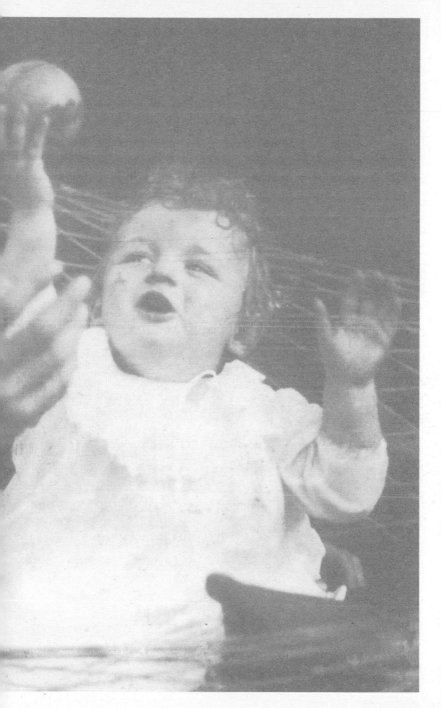

2nd Lieutenant Francis M. Tracy, 91st Division, US, to Gertrude Tracy

The Tracys had been married eleven years and it would seem that he had not been a model husband. This letter of repentance and hope is made all the more poignant by the fact that he was killed seven days later.

France
20 September 1918

Dearest Woman,

Finished your letter last evening, but had to cut it short, as we moved into a new area last night. Have a few moments to spare, so am going to resume my chat with you, the beginning and the end of my temporal ambitions. Perhaps you will consider it an extravagant statement, but it's true, just as true as the fact that during this period of separation, there has come a new strong, more spiritual love into my heart for the dear precious woman who has suffered so much, as I am only now beginning to thoroughly understand, at my hands.

For a person who really desires to see the triumphs of his or her better self, and I confess to such desires, on occasions, war is a wonderful aid. You know there is an old saying, which runs like this, 'When the devil was sick, the devil a monk would be. But when the devil was well, the devil a monk was he', and I believe that mortals are more or less that way, that fear of what may be awaiting them across the 'great divide' makes virtuous men and women, but it isn't fear that I am speaking about now, my girl, but the coming to understand in the midst of almost inconceivable desolation and suffering caused by nothing else but bestial passion, what a mad, devilish thing, uncontrolled passion is, and the indulgence of small whims, is a sad, sad thing as I know now, to my sorrow and everlasting regret. My one prayer is that I may be privileged to have one more opportunity to make you happy. I trust it will be granted me.

Received a letter from you yesterday, enclosing a number of pictures which were taken in Tacoma, and one delightfully sweet one of yourself taken at Salem. You look like a sweet spirit just stepping forth from the dim and distant fifties, or the era of hoops and pantalets. My girl, my girl, how I do miss you. I didn't think it possible for one to be possessed of the longing I have for you. At night I lay awake and think and think of you, the roar of the big guns, giving way before the press of mental pictures of you. I go back and retravel the entire road that we have known together. Back to the old sweetheart days, over ten years ago, the little girl as I first knew her, comes to me again just as wistfully sweet and ingenuous as she was then, all arrayed in white, or pink or lavender, from her little pumps to the hat on her dear shock of gold. Do you remember the frocks? I used to wonder then, if the general color scheme prevailed all the way from the outer garments, thru mysteries of lingerie and laces, to the dearest most ravishingly attractive body that ever set a man's blood on fire.

If I had to go over the same road with you again, I am quite sure the way would be easier for you. The mistakes I have made, the heartaches I have caused you stand out like the shell holes that deface much of this country, that once, was so beautiful. I am learning my lesson, honey, and this experience, this absence from you is burning its brand into my soul, as nothing has ever done before. But God knows I deserve all the punishment I am getting, and I accept it as most penance. I know full well, that it is doing me a world of good. May it continue, until I am safe to be turned loose among civilized peoples. Must break off again. Will continue tomorrow. Good night and God bless and preserve you.

– Write – write. Your devoted Hubby.

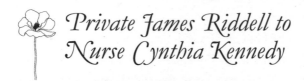

Private James Riddell to Nurse Cynthia Kennedy

James Riddell has fallen in love with his nurse and sends her love letters from his sickbed. 'There is no one on the ward thinks more of you than I do,' he says in another note to her.

His letters are preserved in the Liddle Collection at the University of Leeds, alongside other documents relating to Cynthia's wartime experience. On the back of the photograph of James, she has written: 'James Riddell, Black Watch Regiment. Severe head wound (trepanning). My helpmate in Ward D for many months. Norfolk War Hospital (Military), Thorpe, Nr Norwich'. She didn't reciprocate his feelings, but it is obvious she had a soft spot for him.

Dear Nurse,

I now take the chance of writing you this note to say that I am going to make it my business to see that you don't do so much work on your ward when I get out of bed, you have been so very kind hearted and so awfully good to me that I am going to try and do a little bit for you, I don't give one straw about my self and I am going to see that you don't do too much. I hope you won't keep your promise and say anything to the sister don't forget the old motto nurse ('one good turn deserves another'). I hope you will give me the answer I am expecting to get from you. I have never liked any of the other nurses so much as I have liked you, I would do anything for you with a willing heart, it has always been a great pleasure for me to do ever so little for you, I may have been a little stubborn in some things you have asked me to do, I sincerely hope you will change your mind before I get out of bed and oblige

Your Old Friend

Jock

Don't you think it was me sweeping the ward for you that has made my head bad this time as it was not so. Kindly refrain from thinking so. J. Riddell.

Captain Alfred Bland to Violet Bland

Alfred Bland departed for France with a Manchester regiment in November 1915, leaving behind wife Violet and their two young sons. In early 1916, when he writes this letter, he still finds war a thrill and separation bearable. And yet it doesn't feel as if he loves his wife any the less for that.

My only and eternal blessedness,

I wonder whether you resent my cheerfulness ever! Do you, dear? Because you might, you know. I ought, by all the rules of love, to spend my days and nights in an eternity of sighs and sorrow for our enforced parting. And by all the rules of war, I ought to be enduring cold and hardship, hunger and fatigue, bitterness of soul and dismay of heart. Alas! what shall I say in my defence? Because not even Merriman can depress me, and as for the C.O., I am simply impertinent to him, while the dull routine of being behind the line fills me with an inexhaustible supply of cheerful patience. What shall we say about it? Would it rejoice you if I confessed to being utterly miserable every now and then? If I told you how I loathed war and hated every minute that prolonged it? if I admitted that I yearn hourly for my return, my final return away from it all? if I said that I hated my brother officers and was sick of the sight of the Company?

if I described the filthy squalor of the village streets, the sickening repetition of low clouds and sulky drizzle and heavy rain, and the dreary monotony of ration beef and ration bread. Would you be glad or sorry? Oh! I <u>know</u> how sympathetic and sad you would feel, and I <u>know</u> you would <u>not</u> be glad at all. Would you? And if you <u>were</u> glad, you would be all wrong; because, even if these things were true, it wouldn't bring us together again, it wouldn't make me love you more, it wouldn't sweeten those embraces we are deprived of for the moment, it wouldn't strengthen our divine oneness one scrap. Would it? No, my Darling, thank the heavens daily that in all circumstances you will be right in picturing your boy out here simply brimming over with gaiety irrepressible. I am becoming a byword. Cushion says 'I <u>like</u> you, Bill Bland.' Why? because I am always laughing at everybody and everything, greeting the seen and the unseen with a cheer. And it isn't a pose. It's the solemn truth. So let us go back again to those imaginary admissions above. I am <u>never</u> utterly miserable, not even when I yearn most for the touch of your lips and a sight of my boys. Why? because I am in France, where the war is, and I know I ought to be here. And I don't loathe war, I love 95% of it, and hate the thought of it being ended too soon. And I don't yearn hourly for my final return, although I am very pleasantly excited at the possibility of 9 days leave in March, which indeed we haven't earned by any means so far. And I don't loathe my brother officers but love them more than I had dreamed possible, and as for my Company, why, bless it! And the mud is such friendly mud, somehow, so yielding and considerate – and I don't have to clean my own boots. And I have lost the habit of regarding the weather, for if it rains, we get wet, and if it doesn't, we don't, and if the sun shines, how nice! And as for our food, well, I've given you an idea of that before, and I have nothing to add to the statements made in this House on November 30 and December 6 last or any other time. No, dear whether you like it or not, I am fundamentally happy and on the surface childishly gay. And there's an end on't.

Post just going. Good night, darling.

Ever your

Alfred

Nurse Betty Robinson to Private Robert Galbraith

In April 1916, Robert Galbraith had an attack of appendicitis whilst at training camp in Berkhampstead. In the local hospital, Betty Robinson nursed him back to health. They began writing to each other as soon as Robert had recovered and left for France. Their romance progressed quickly and can be measured in Betty's letters by the growing affection in her salutation, from 'Dear Mr Galbraith', 'My Dear Mr Galbraith', 'Dear Robert', 'My Dear Robert', 'My Dearest Robert', to, finally, 'My Own Darling'.

The letter is undated but was probably written early in 1917

Nurses Home
West Herts Hospital
Hemel Hempstead

My Own Darling,

Thanks so much for your last letter received this morning. I do appreciate your letters so. Although I never look for them and if I don't get one well it isn't so disappointing and then if I do get one it's rare. Sometimes I have it in my pocket unopened. Haven't time to read it till I get off-duty. Fancy keeping it from 8 am till 2 pm. But still I would rather, then I can enjoy it. Have you had a very boring time, darling?

Thanks for saying I'm too sensible to worry about you. Well I think it's true in a way because I'm not. Perhaps it is because I don't realize the danger. But don't tell me anything about that. Let me stay blissfully ignorant. I'm still plodding on in the same old way. Sweeping, dusting, tending to Casualties, getting Tommies their teas etc. Today has been quite busy for Sunday. Well darling, it's dim and time the light was out in here, so goodbye sweetheart and the best of luck to you.

Heaps of love and kisses, your own Betty

Private Marin Guillaumont to Marguerite Guillaumont

In 1914, Marin and Marguerite Guillaumont had been married four years when Marin, a primary school teacher, joined the army. Marguerite gave birth to a daughter, their first child, in December that year. The baby was named Lucile but then became known affectionately as Luciole, the French word for 'tracer bullet'. Over the next ten days, Marin wrote three letters to Marguerite, and each one is very tender and brimming with pride.

14 December 1914
8 o'clock in the evening

My very dear one

I have received your telegram. How happy, and anxious, I am. How are you, darling, how is our little girl? Did you suffer much? Were you able to get a doctor? Had you managed to find a wet-nurse? The telegram is very short.

How I long for details. I'm worried about so many things. The state of mind in which you have been living for the past four and a half months might have had an unhappy influence. Worrying might hurt the baby. Stay brave my darling. Think of our little daughter: what name have you given her? Tell me her name soon. How I long to see her, how impatient I am to come home. But my return is still far off, several months at least.

Tell me about her in detail as soon as you can. Tell me everything. I hope I will see her. I want to see her. How I wish she had been born a year earlier. Get them to send me lots of writing paper so that I can write you a long letter.

Every time that I can't do it, kiss her for me. I'm sure I won't sleep tonight. But don't worry: I won't be unhappy, although I am anxious: if any complications arise, you won't find it easy to get a doctor and there are hardly any chemists.

Tell me that our child will live, I'm so eager to know that. Those poor little things are so delicate. It takes so little. I'm hoping. What colour are her eyes? What are her little hands like?

Will she be pretty? How I wish that she shall look like you. Alas, I won't be able to see her when she is tiny. I love you, do you see, I love her as much as I love you. Tell me, let me hear lots and lots about her. Does she cry a lot? And you, are you in pain, darling? Were you able to write the telegram yourself: no, I'm sure someone must have signed it on your behalf to reassure me. But why would things go wrong? Haven't we got enough trials without that? Everything is fine, isn't it?

You must give me good news.

As soon as you can, write to me, a long letter.

Where will I be by then? Somewhere on the front; it goes all the way from Switzerland to the North Sea. Each of us is just an atom. But if all goes well I will survive, I'm sure of it. I'm keeping all my wits about me; we will be very happy, yes, later, in a few months, we're earning the right to that now. I haven't seen our child, I want to see the child and I'm firmly convinced that I shall. I have to, don't I? Keep my letters, if I were to not come back she can read them later, and she'll know that her daddy loved her very much.

Teach her to be good and unaffected. As she grows up and is able to understand you, teach her everything, don't be afraid to talk to her about the ugly side of life, so that she won't be taken unawares and won't make anyone suffer.

Never allow her to be a gossip about others. I would like her to learn music and foreign languages, without those we aren't complete beings. But why am I telling you all this, you know it as well as I do and then we will both be there together, of course. While waiting for me to come back love her a lot, double, for you and for me, and tell me quickly what her name is. I would like something like a Lucienne, Yvonne, Marguerite, Marcelle, Germaine.

Or, I don't know, give her an English name. There are some nice ones. But it's all done and dusted anyway, I love her whatever her name is. I'm just so eager to know what it is, that's all.

How I would love to be near you to look after you myself, to cuddle her to sleep, and to think that even after I get back I'll still have to live apart from her, but the hope that she will live will be even stronger. I'm mad. I interrupt my writing to say I have a daughter: 'I've got a daughter'. How wonderful that is to say: I can see her already a bit older, I seem to see her coming home from school with you.

Do you see, if I don't come back, I will still have lived her whole life. I feel as if I'm already following her through her life. But by the time you get this letter, what will she be? If you were in Paris I would get myself taken there to see her. If only it were possible to have a photo. How I would love to see her when she's so, so tiny. If everything's going well, you must be very happy: give yourself completely over to her; she's your first concern from now on, if I was gone from you, you would only have her to sweeten your life: a mother and her daughter, when they love each other, should not and cannot ever be unhappy.

20 December 1914

I already love her, our little Lucile, do you see; I dream about her; I've seen her already as tall as little Camille; she was wearing a white coat with a white ribbon in her hair. Oh, how I loved her like that; she seemed as gentle as her name. You'll see how good she will be for you, for us both. When she's bigger, you'll tell her that, won't you!

I've never loved you as much as since the day when you told me, a little before the Easter holidays, that you thought you were expecting. What crazy nights and crazy kisses beforehand; what memories that child represents. What unbridled love does that child sum up, and also how much we love her and will love her, our poor star of these trench nights.

Oh, she is so pretty our Lucile; I spent the night looking at her photo by the light of the moon while I was on guard; today, I'm forever pulling it out of the envelope; the picture is in front of me as I write to you. I'm also looking at your picture; I'm comparing them. Think of last spring; of all those hours we spent delightfully entwined together; isn't it true that our Luciole was already calling to us her right to live, was throwing us into each other's arms, begging us to create her? Now we have her. She is ours, really ours, no one's but ours. May her life be easy.

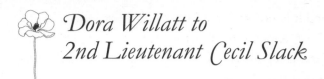

Dora Willatt to
2nd Lieutenant Cecil Slack

Dora Willatt and Cecil Slack had known each other since childhood, in Hull, East Yorkshire, and were just good friends when Cecil volunteered in 1914. Two years later, Dora still thought of him as her 'best boy friend', and so his out-of-the-blue proposal of marriage quite unseated her.

Silkstone [nr Barnsley]
7.6.16

My dear Cecil,

I have come into that little wood and am sitting under a tree only about ten yards away from where we sat together and you asked me to marry you. I couldn't write in the house – I felt as if I were nearer to you if I came away from everybody and am absolutely by myself. It was a very great surprise and even a shock when you told me you loved me and I had not the slightest idea you were going to tell me so then. I am going to tell you the absolute truth and just write down as I think – I mean as thoughts come into my head, and when you write back to me I want you to do exactly the same – don't keep back anything whatever your thoughts may be about me.

I must say that I have thought of you as my best boy

friend and it is not because I have known you practically as long as I can remember – it is for yourself. Betty Sowerbutts did tell me at Penrhos that you were keen on me but I'm afraid at that time I didn't think anything about you – when I left school I liked you just as I liked my other friends and it was not until after you were wounded last year and you came to our house a good deal for tennis that I liked you more than the others who came.

You will notice I am saying 'liking' – I have never thought whether I loved you or not – I knew you liked me, somehow, but I had not thought you loved me – it is why I had not thought of it so much, that it has been so hard to see if my 'liking' for you had turned into love for you. I remember dreaming, one night since we came here, that you were married to another girl and I remember waking up with a miserable, hopeless feeling.

Before I say any more I want you to think whether you yourself are quite sure you love me, and that when you asked me to marry you you were not influenced by any excitement of the moment – because you had not seen me for some time or because you were just going away.

Have you yourself quite made up your mind about me – have you thought everything over and what it all means? Think very carefully indeed – you would see me every morning first, last thing every night – same face behind the coffee-pot every breakfast, same face behind the tea-pot every tea-time – when you holiday you would holiday with me. Think of it – and then think if you had got the wrong girl how awful it would be – it would be tragic – nothing is so awful as domestic unhappiness and quarrelling. My ideal man and woman are those who give themselves whole-heartedly to each other with all their love and who help each other and go close through life. Cecil, do think it over well – we are still very young and you seem young to want to be engaged – altho' I'm glad you're older than I am. You know you haven't met so many girls and I am one of the very few girls you know thoroughly.

When I went to bed I overheard Father tell Mother that your affaire you are going to do out there was jolly risky – I began to think and then realized if you never came back and I never saw you again – what I should do and what I should feel like. It is horrible of me to talk like this but I am telling you all – it made me realize that I do love you Cecil – oh, that I could see you again now – but I cannot tell if I love you as much as you love me. How much do you love me Cecil? It is awfully hard to tell when one has not been thinking about it long.

I should like to get to know you yourself better and then at the end of six months if I am quite sure of my own mind and I have that sacred love for you that only man and woman can have I would promise definitely to become your wife – until then let us have an understanding between each other and write to each other and keep nothing back and hide nothing. If at any time you or I meet someone that we should like better I shall not hesitate to tell you and you must promise that you will tell me – of course if we were to get married we should know our own minds whoever we came in contact with, and be true – absolutely true – I swear I would Cecil – as long as we both lived.

I do want you to be careful when your little 'affaire' comes off next week. Will you try and remember to take care of yourself – you are very brave Cecil to be so cheerful over it – I simply couldn't do it or stand it at the front – I must be a coward. Don't do anything rash, please, and write to me before it comes off.

If you think differently from what you told me on Monday do be sure and tell me and we will carry on as before and be chums and I will be just the same to you.

Goodbye, Cecil, and remember I have some love for you,
Dora

And his reply:

В.Е.Г.

My dear Dora,

For a long time before asking you to marry me I had been thinking things over and I was and am quite certain of my own feelings. But I feel a rotter for asking you when I did. I ought to have waited, for one thing, until the war was over, and for another until I had more idea of your feelings. As it is I have given you a shock and have kindled feelings which should not have been aroused. I am sorry and yet I am glad.

You asked me to be quite sure I was not influenced by any excitement of the moment. I was not. When I came out on

Monday I had not any definite intention, but I had a sort of hazy wondering as to whether I should ask you to be my wife. You think that you brought me away from the other two – I think the shoe was on the other foot. When I suggested that we should go back to look for them I had not the slightest intention of finding them. I only wanted to make our walk a little longer, and to sum up my courage.

Get rid of the idea that I acted on the impulse of the moment. I have loved you ever since I was at Rydal. A schoolboy love then – it often happens to schoolboys and then dies out. Mine did not die.

As time went on I did not see you much, the flame died down a little with occasional flarings up, but I always intended some day to ask you to marry me.

When I was wounded and was in Hospital in London, my Mother told me that your Mother was in London with you and Flossie, and I took it as confirmation of what I already seemed to know.

It was after seeing you that day, I think it was a Monday, May 10th, that I knew my schoolboy love was real true honest Love for you. You say you will let me know if you come across anyone whom you 'like' better than me. You ask me to do the same. I promise – and it's a very easy promise too, for there will be no-one. I know.

You ask me how much I love you. All I can say is that I just love you with my whole heart. I love you together with my Mother and my Father and my honour, but on a different scale altogether.

There is just one thing I want to mention before I forget it, and it is this – if I should by any chance be crippled I shall cry off everything. I would not dream of marrying if I had not a sound body. That is one reason why I'm such a rotter for having asked you in the middle of the war. Perhaps it would be better if we put aside what has happened until after the war?

About this little 'affaire' that will be coming off soon – it is not nearly as dangerous as one would expect. One hears every day of a successful raid. I shall do my utmost to get back whole. I am much too fond of life to run unnecessary risks.

Goodbye,

Love from Cecil

As Dora suggested, they waited six months to be sure of their feelings, and then they went ahead with their engagement. Cecil survived the war and they married in 1919.

Helen Muriel Harpin to 2nd Lieutenant Charles L. Overton (Neville)

Muriel Harpin met Neville Overton in 1916 when he was on convalescent leave at her aunt's house in Southport, England. Muriel was also on war service, nursing at a nearby military hospital. Their relationship went from strength to strength, no doubt sustained by her irresistible letters.

Here, two years later, Neville is once again recovering from an illness. Having been sent back to England, he is waiting to be released from a London hospital. 'I __am__ longing to see you, dear,' writes Muriel, ' – please don't be any thinner.'

3.10.18

Neville my darling,

I am getting more and more excited at the thought of seeing you on Tuesday. What are we going to do with Mother? We <u>must</u> lose her sometimes! She wants to go and see the Aldriches in Wimbledon one day and another day she is going to some people who live in Kensington, but she won't want to be out late in the evening on her wild lone (unfortunately). <u>What</u> shall we do? I keep thinking of taxis for <u>one</u> thing. One can have lots of kisses in a taxi when needs must! Aren't I getting depraved? But I'm longing so much for a good time and I <u>do</u> love <u>your</u> kisses. I don't think I could ever tire of them, and we can't go a whole 3 days without any, can we? On the other hand we can't leave Mother stranded the <u>whole</u> time and go to theatres and leave her behind always. I foresee some complications. I suppose it will have to be matinees if we go to theatres. How often can you have a pass till 10 pm? I don't care what we do so long as we're together, but I do mean to enjoy every bit just as much as possible. I <u>am</u> longing to see you, dear – please don't be any thinner.

Night duty now, so goodnight my very own Boy. Be good till I come!

Heaps and heaps of love,

Always your

Muriel

Cicely Marriott to Lieutenant Colonel Sidney Marriott

This is a tiny letter, written on a very flimsy piece of paper. The last paragraph of the letter is smudged, as if it has got wet at some point, and a small (approximately 3 inch by 2 inch) photograph of Cicely in the garden has become stuck to it. He most likely kept this folded up in his wallet, along with a newspaper cutting of the announcement of the birth.

6/8/15

My darling husband

A very special favour by the nurse. I may just write one sheet.

You will have had the wire by now. Your little daughter is a perfect darling exactly like you with black black hair and blue eyes. She has such pretty little features, your mouth exactly. I do wish you could see us both. I have had her in bed with me all afternoon as good as gold.

I am so happy, darling, & feel very well.

It is wonderful to think that after all this long waiting, the little thing is really here. She is having her bath now, such a dear tiny little morsel. The nurse is sweet & so kind and the doc only just arrived in time, but giving me chloroform put it back one and a half hours.

I would give anything to have you here now, the darling little baby sends her father & my darling husband [all our love]. At 6 lbs 9 ozs, she weighs more than babies usually are. She is screaming now in her bath . . . rather than being dressed.

With all my love, my darling
your loving wife,
Cicely

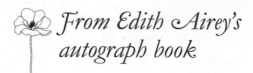

From Edith Airey's autograph book

Edith Airey was on war work on a dairy farm in Easton in Suffolk, where she met a convalescing Scottish soldier from the nearby Red Cross hospital. It seems likely they had a flirtation and nothing more, and the poem he wrote in her autograph book when he left, maybe to return to the Front, certainly makes no promises, but is rather lovely and hopeful all the same.

If I ever join in wedlock,
And the chances are but few,
I would wed you, Edith Airey,
Or a girl the same as you.
And when the war is over,
And vanquished are our foes,
I will come back to Easton
And wed my English rose.
Then through life's dark journey,
We everything will share.
The thistle and the English rose
Will make a happy pair.

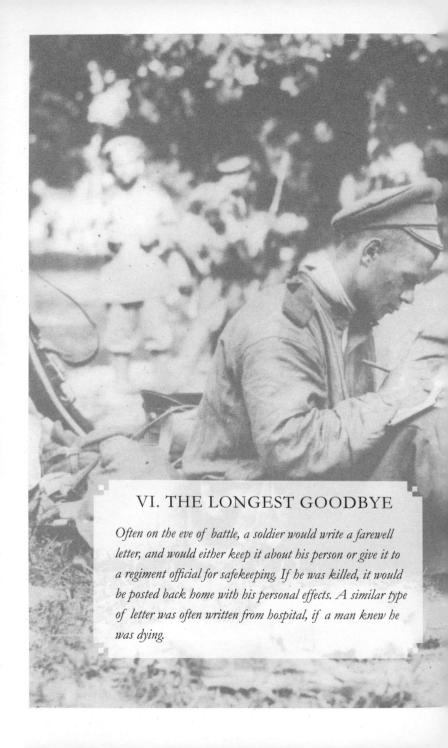

VI. THE LONGEST GOODBYE

Often on the eve of battle, a soldier would write a farewell letter, and would either keep it about his person or give it to a regiment official for safekeeping. If he was killed, it would be posted back home with his personal effects. A similar type of letter was often written from hospital, if a man knew he was dying.

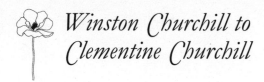

Winston Churchill to
Clementine Churchill

On 17 July 1915, Winston Churchill wrote the following letter and sealed it in an envelope marked, 'To be sent to Mrs Churchill in the event of my death'.

Do not grieve for me too much. I am a spirit confident of my rights. Death is only an incident & not the most important which happens to us in this state of being. On the whole, especially since I met you my darling I have been happy, & you have taught me how noble a woman's heart can be. If there is anywhere else I shall be on the look out for you. Meanwhile look forward, feel free, rejoice in life, cherish the children, guard my memory. God bless you.

    Good bye.

        W.

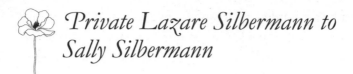

Private Lazare Silbermann to Sally Silbermann

The Silbermanns were Romanian refugees settled in France. Lazare Silbermann volunteered for active service as soon as war was declared but before he left for the Front, he wrote this 'testamentary' letter to his wife and four children.

Lazare survived the war but was one of the first victims of the Spanish influenza after the Armistice.

Paris, 7 August 1914

My dear Sally

Before I set off to do my duty towards our adopted country – France, of which we have never had any cause for complaint – I have another duty: to give you some advice, for I don't know whether I shall ever return. If you are reading this letter, of course, I will be gone, because it is stipulated that you can only open it after my death: 1) you will find in the safe four letters, which you must pass on to the people named on them, 2) you will find an official document setting out my assets and liabilities and which confirms that you and our dear children are the sole heirs of the miserable little lot that remains of me. Of course, my dear, I realize that I am leaving you in poverty because all this looks quite good, but in reality has no substance. I leave you a heavy burden, which is the bringing up of four small orphans whom I would have wanted to see happy, because, as you know, I have never done anything solely for my own benefit. I have always thought about how to make you, and our children, happy. I did everything I could for that goal, but in the end, I haven't managed to achieve what I wanted. Thank you for the few years of happiness which you have given me since our marriage – alas, too short – and I beg you to be brave, very brave to bring up our little cherubs and inspire them with honesty and loyalty, giving them yourself as their example, and I am convinced you will not lack that courage. Keep telling them about the sacrifices beyond the call of duty which I made for them, and that they should follow my example. As for you, I think you will have fond memories of me. We have loved each other till the end, and it's this memory, along with that of my conduct towards you and everyone else that will give you the courage to bear the heavy burden which I am leaving you. One last time, I charge you to guard jealously the honour of our dear children by setting them good examples, and I am sure these will find their echo when the moment comes.

I kiss you one last time.

Your companion in fortune and misfortune.

Lazare

My dear little children,

I have one final piece of advice to give you. Today, you are young; tomorrow you will be grown-ups. Please think about what I am writing to you here. Respect your mother; always obey her for she bears the heavy responsibility of being both mother and father. Use both of us as your example. Love each other, be loyal and honest, and you will be happy with a clear conscience. You, Rosette, my dear child, must set an example to Ernestine, your little sister, and to Jean and Charles, your little brothers, so that you all stay on the true path. All of you, be good children. I hope that the tears I am shedding as I write this letter will inspire you to do all that I would wish and become everything that I would hope for you.

Keep this letter carefully, preserve the memory of your unfortunate father and follow his advice.

Lazare Silbermann

PS Most of all, respect your mother. Shield her from any pain that may come her way. Make her life easier and help her to forget any bitterness that life may bring her.

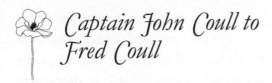

Captain John Coull to Fred Coull

John Coull's farewell letter to his son was forwarded to the family after he was killed in action on 30 September 1918.

France

2.4.17

1pm

My dear boy Fred,

This is a letter you will never see unless your daddy falls in the field. It is his farewell words to you in case anything happens. My boy I love you dearly and would have greatly liked to get leave for a few days to kiss you and shake hands again, after a few months separation, but as this seems at the moment unlikely, I drop you these few lines to say 'God bless you' and keep you in the true brave manly upright course which I would like to see you follow.

You will understand better as you get older that your daddy came out to France for your sakes and for our Empire's sake. If he died it was in a good cause and all I would ask of you, dear boy, is that you will keep this note in memory of me, and throughout your life may all that is good attend you and influence you. May you be strong to withstand the temptations of life and when you come to the evening of your days you are able to say with St Paul, 'I have fought the good fight.'

Goodbye dear boy and if it is that we are not to meet again in this life, may it be certain that we shall meet in another life to come, which faith I trust you will hold on to and live up to.

I remain ever

Your loving Daddy

J. F. Coull

Gunner Frank Bracey to Win

Frank Bracey wrote this goodbye letter to his sweetheart when he was on leave. He seemed to have had a foreboding that he would not return to England, and he was proved right, for he was killed three months later. The letter is said to be tear-stained.

May 5 16
8 Hill St

Dearest Win

I am writing just a line Win in case of accidents. Just to let you know how I have allways loved you Dear. You are the best little girl on God's earth have I told you before. But I am writing this because I have a feeling that I shall not come back again. I have most of your letters in this box Dear and I wish you to have them and the cards. You may think I am a bit taped writing this dear but I cannot help it. If I do come back dearest you will never see this letter but I have a strong feeling today that I shall never see England again. In case I do pop under the earth I want you to be happy and look out for a worthier chap than your Humble, you have been every thing to me Win. I know your love is mine forever dearest but if I do not come back I wish you the best of happiness and a good husband. I know you told me what you would do for yourself if I did not return but Win for the sake of our love I wish you to be brave, it would be hard for you little girl I know, but do nothing of the kind. My last wish is that you marry a good man and to be happy and to think of your Humble now and then. I felt I must write these few lines Win but whatever happens dear just keep a stout heart and think that your Frank did his bit for the women of this little isle. I expect you will think your Humble crazy but I was never saner than I am now.

Frank

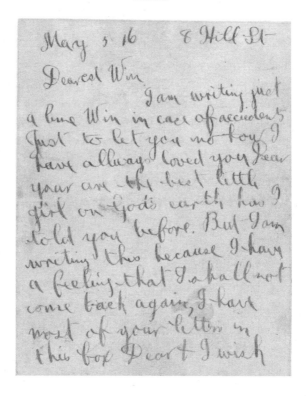

Sergeant Francis Gautier to Marie Gautier

Francis Gautier had been seriously wounded and as he lay dying in the military hospital in Earls Colne, Essex, he wrote this letter to his young daughter. In the Imperial War Museum in London, the Gautier file contains this letter and also a postcard, sent to Marie by her brother, who died at Ypres. It was Marie's wish that this letter be preserved alongside her brother's postcard.

2 April 1916

To my darling daughter Marie,

Dearly loved daughter. This, my letter to you, is written in grief. I had hoped to spend many happy years with you after the War was over and to see you grow up into a good and happy woman. I am writing because I want you in after years to know how dearly I loved you, I know that you are too young now to keep me in your memory. I know your dear mother will grieve, be a comfort to her, remember when you are old enough that she lost her dear brave son, your brother, and me your father within a short time. Your brother was a dear brave boy, honour his memory for he loved you, and your brothers dearly and he died like a brave soldier in defence of his home and Country. May God guide and keep you safe and that at last we may all meet together in His eternal rest. I am your loving & affectionate father,

F. H. Gautier xxxxxxxxxxxxxxxxxxxxxx

VII. DARK DAYS

Fear, helplessness, jealousy, temptation and the trauma of terrible things witnessed – the mental anguish of those at home as well as at the Front couldn't always be kept under control and sometimes spilled over. Letters written under these circumstances were cathartic and could avert a deeper crisis, but many signalled the end; matters had gone too far.

Thomas Rentoul to Ivy

Thomas Rentoul was an army chaplain. He had met Ivy when he was training to be a minister in Melbourne and boarding with a couple and their daughter – Ivy. When he left for France in 1916, they had just become engaged, and Ivy's parents did not approve of the match. Thomas was in his early thirties, Ivy was about seventeen, a music student. The letter to which he now writes in reply seems to have precipitated a crisis, and it follows very swiftly on from an earlier crisis of faith, when he felt he was putting his love for Ivy before his love for God.

9/12/16
France

Dear Ivy,

Yours of Oct. 25th came tonight. Oh what shall I say? The words of it burned my brain like fire. After kneeling down to ask God's help, I found He had provided some help even before I asked. It was a hospital notice. So I am just back from a visit to a dying boy. In trying to comfort him, I have found some rest for my own poor heart. He will die tomorrow. He will then <u>know.</u> <u>We</u> only grope and disquiet ourselves in vain. And the thought will keep rushing into my head as it did when I looked into his patient smiling eyes

– would to God that we could change places! He is quite young and <u>handsome</u> and probably has some girl who loves him truly. But he will die and I must live. I wonder why I ever loved you. I wonder why I do now? I don't know and it's no use wondering; I do love you fervently, passionately still. And I will ever love you. I know I am not fit to live, and you may probably be happier, and <u>other people</u> be better pleased if you marry someone else, but even that knowledge cannot and does not abate my love. I want you and need you! It is only a merciful and wise God who knows what the end will be. For two things <u>only</u> I am glad: First, that you were faithful to our compact and told me <u>all</u>. And second, that God gave me the chance to be away from you for so long – that you may be able to <u>choose</u> freely, apart from my influence. I would rather you be someone else's, rather than not be freely and unreservedly mine. You do not say how the invitation came nor what the party was about, but I am accustomed to read your letters with my imagination, and it looks to me somewhat like a 'trap' for Ivy. You are a woman. When this reaches you, you will be nearing your 18th birthday. <u>You must not be influenced</u>. Remember you have to live your own life. So knowing how busy you have been and knowing how people rig these little things up, and remembering how you were always prone to make too much of people at first acquaintance, I can make <u>allowance</u>. But even if I could not make allowance, I could forgive. Love cannot help but forgive and I love you with my whole heart.

Last night the Colonel and a few of us were sitting round

the fire: one fellow got a bundle of letters – they were from his mother, sisters and mates. They mentioned four cases of girls who had proved untrue to their soldier lovers. These were all officers known to us and by some perversity of fate our best officers. These girls had become engaged to some cold-footed cowards who had not enough manhood to enlist. Some of these poor officers have had bullets through them, been wasted by disease, in hospital: out again healed and strong and are now back in France, fighting that the Australian girls and women may not be subjected to the foul infamy and disgrace brought upon the women and girls of Belgium, Serbia, Roumania and Poland, by German and Austrian swine! And while we are here, in this rotten life (and in France it is hellish) the girls must have some admirers and pick up any loafing coward.

If only you could have seen the faces of these few officers as they spoke of these things! Black and terrible! And hear their awful words as they said, 'Poor old Fred' or 'Poor old George'. You are very young, Ive. You do not get the right point of view always, but I cannot imagine you becoming one of that shallow class of girls who are faithless and impatient. Now God bless you and teach you. Religion does not consist in sentiment or beautiful words, or music or sermons but in principle. You will be honourable in future Ive to yourself. You owe it to your sweet self not to do anything that will cause you any bitter confusion afterwards.

And now I will go to bed – but perhaps not to sleep. The bright eyes of that dying boy are upon me. The hurt caused by your letter is as deep as the love I bear you. But tonight ends that forever and I will try to trust you as before. I have had a hard week. Our poor boys are suffering dreadfully for the effects of the cold. Many more will die. I had a funeral yesterday, one today and one on Tuesday.

I wonder if your love for me is growing cold. If it is, how can I regain it, kindle it? I do not know. I have asked you about how long you think I ought to stay, I have asked you about sending a ring for April 16th – but to these questions I have had no answer. Perhaps they are not fair – oh perhaps, perhaps, it's all perhaps and wonderings and hopes and despair. If I could get so that I didn't care I would be at rest. Now I must not write any more or I may put something unkind. I write all this out of my heart, in deep distress and perplexity. By this mail a couple of parcels arrived. The room is littered with soaps, toothbrushes, sox, mittens, lollies, potted ham, cocoa, hankies and a collection of odds and ends – and by a strange freak a lovely suede-bound copy of that sad poem of Tennyson's – Evangeline. One parcel was from Gertie Hawkins and the other from the Hamilton girls at Wynard. I have never written to any of these girls. I wonder why they are so kind and mindful of me. For your sake, I have ceased writing to several who were always so good to me, but I will just send them a card of thanks. The pile of articles is meaningless to me tonight. I wish they were not here. I don't want them. I do want the kindness they represent.

       Thomas

A wife to her husband,
a prisoner of war

*We don't know anything more about this unfortunate couple, but
the strain of separation has brought the wife to breaking point.
Whether she carried out her threat, we'll never know.*

Gleiwitz

Upper Silesia

April 1917

Dear Husband!

This is the last letter I am writing to you, because on the
24th I am going to marry another man. Then, I don't have to
work any longer. I have already been working for three years
as long as you are away from home. All other men come
home for leave, only you POWs never come. Nobody knows
how long it will take until you come home. That's why I am
going to have a new husband. I will give the children to the
orphanage. I don't give a rat's ass about a life like that! There
is no way to survive with these few Pfennig benefits. At work
they have a big mouth about the women. Now I don't need
to go to work, now the other man is going to work for me.
All wives whose husbands are POWs will do the same thing
and they will all get rid of the children. Three years of work

are too much for the women and 20 Mark for benefit and 10 Mark child benefit are not enough. One cannot live on that. Everything is so expensive now. One pound of bacon costs 8 Mark, a shirt 9 Mark.

Your wife

Private Maurice Drans to Georgette Clabault

Maurice Drans was from Fresnay-sur-Sarthe in France and met Georgette when he was on leave. They became engaged in 1916 and did eventually marry, but the marriage did not last. Like many soldiers returning to civilian life, he became unstable, no doubt affected by his war experiences. In this love letter of sorts, more cathartic than romantic, he doesn't spare her from the horror.

17 May 1917

My dear Georgette,

The day before yesterday, in the evening – in the inky-blue night – I encountered on earth signs from the next life. The scene was like a macabre, sparsely populated cemetery: no shelter, no headstones, abandoned by all human life, an open mine of innumerable scattered corpses without tombs, a mass grave open to the crawling worms and the ceaseless rain of shells. There were more than a thousand bodies there, twisted and torn to pieces, heaped one upon another.

I was straggling through the night near the lines, my burden of firearms on my back; I kept stumbling; my mouth, my nostrils were full of that taste, that smell; the enemy and the Frenchman empathizing in one final rictus, in the embrace of their violated naked flesh; jumbled up, mingled on this plain of ghoulish madness, in this abyss strafed by constant noisy fire. Germans and Frenchmen rotting one on top of the other, with not the slightest hope of burial by friendly or pious hands. Retrieving the dead means adding your own corpse to that gaping grave, for war is insatiable. Every night, we walk the length of this frozen hell populated by ghosts, sick at heart, blocking our noses, lips pursed. O my Georgette, I should be talking to you about love, and instead I'm telling you about this! But the worst of all is that when we get back, after midnight, we eat – the only meal we'll get in twenty-four hours – with our mouths still full of the dead; we eat blindly without so much as a glimmer of light.

Ah! It won't go down and it's cold, congealed, unappetising.

Maurice

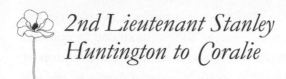

2nd Lieutenant Stanley Huntington to Coralie

Stanley Huntington and Coralie were from the small town of Waverley in New Zealand. Coralie was very young, only seventeen years old, when she met Stanley in June 1917. When he enlisted and was sent to a training camp, they began to write to each other. Theirs was a tentative relationship, rather cool on her part. He sent her a sweetheart brooch and declared his love for her, and when he passed his officers exams, he even tried to impress her with his new rank, but it was to no avail and her letters became less frequent. By the time his regiment set sail for Europe, several of his letters had gone unanswered.

Somewhere at sea

16th December, 1917

To still my best girlie,

Well Coralie dear, this is my third letter to you since leaving N.Z. & you are still as addressed above – have you any remarks to make?

Since last writing we have had some thrilling adventures & seen wonderful sights. Scenery never to be forgotten & incidents which seem strangely like moving pictures have implanted themselves upon my memory. The weather has been very calm, warm, & settled, with the exception of last night. Iced water & lashings of ice-cream have made their appearance, much to our joy. However we are now running into colder weather & shortly we shall be digging into our trunks for warmer wearing apparel. In N.Z. you will be just commencing your summer. Our summer this year will be a very short one, much to our regret.

Last night was the roughest & wildest we have yet experienced. The old boat pitched & tossed & shipped a few seas in great style. In the middle of this gale, something went wrong with the electricity & the steamer's whistle commenced blowing at top speed. Everyone thought it was a real alarm & scared & white faces showed up everywhere. People were rushing about as if the day of judgement had arrived. Your ownest own was safely in bed & did not hurry out. I have come to the conclusion that if the boat really does go down it is better to light a cigarette & calmly sit by and watch the spectacle.

Well, Coralie, how's things & how am I standing with you now kiddie. In your last letters you have never written to me personally, & I am simply dying to know your thoughts concerning me. Do please hurry & tell me & be sure that when you do tell me that it is something nice. You don't know how I miss you dearest – do you miss me at all? I am wondering whether you ever want me like you used to or whether you ever will. Perhaps, eh!

Well, dearest, we are drawing nearer to our destination. We are now on the other side of the world & you are further away than ever. Do think of me sometimes & then perhaps our thoughts will be transmuted. I have still your photo, in which you look so archly at me. You look unutterable things, things that I some day hope you will look for me alone.

So kiddie, write & comfort me because I deserve it, but greatest because you want to, & tell me that you want to.

Goodnight, beloved, may the twinkling stars above look down and caress you in my stead; may they plead for me.

With the greatest love,

Stan x

Emily Chitticks to
Private William Martin

Emily Chitticks met William Martin in August 1916 and two months later, they were engaged. In January 1917, he went with his Devonshire regiment to France and they continued their romance through their frequent loving letters. In late March 1917, Emily grew anxious that she hadn't heard from him in a while, but then a letter arrived and she was reassured. In her reply (the letter quoted here), she is relieved that he is still 'quite alright', but he isn't – he was killed on the 27th. For some inexplicable reason, this and all her subsequent letters to him are written in red ink. All are returned to her, with 'Killed in Action' scrawled across the envelope.

29/3/17

My Dearest Will,

I was so delighted to get your letter this morning & to know you are quite alright. I am pleased to say I am alright myself & I hope dear this will find you the same. I was so pleased to hear darling that you had such a nice enjoyable evening. It was quite a treat I am sure. I don't suppose you do get much amusement. It helps to make the time a bit less monotonous when you have anything like that. I am glad you are getting my letters dear, I am not waiting until I get your letters now dear before I write because it would make it so long for you to wait for a letter. I can understand darling your not being able to write as frequently. I shall get used to waiting for your letters soon I guess, but at first it seems so strange after being used to having them so regularly. Mrs T & I have been out in the garden today, we are getting quite expert, we have been digging & sowing onions & leeks.

Arthur told me tonight that people in the village are saying that he is 'my young man.' Did you ever hear anything so ridiculous. I believe it's him that's been putting it about, a nasty young scamp. If it comes to my ears that he has he'll get it pretty hot. Isn't it dreadful Will the lies people put about. But I can't help laughing. Fancy him for a young man. I should think. His face is enough to give any girl a bilious attack. If ever I detested a fellow it's him. He seems to be full of nothing but lies & deceit. I only wish to goodness he would clear out, he ought to be at the front it would do him good. Well darling, I don't know any more to say now. I am feeling sleepy. Oh I wish you were here darling, but it's no good wishing. Fondest love and lots of kisses from

Your Everloving Little Girl

Emily

xxxxxxxxxxxx

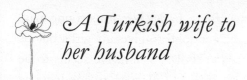

A Turkish wife to her husband

This letter was found on the body of a Turkish soldier killed at Gallipoli.

To my dear Husband,

I humbly beg to enquire after your blessed health. Your daughter sends her special salaams, and kisses your hands. Since you left I have seen no one. Since your departure I have had no peace. Your mother has not ceased to weep since you left. We are all in a bad way. Your wife says to herself 'While my husband was here we had some means' since your departure we have received nothing at all. Please write quickly and send what you can. All your friends kiss your hands and your feet.

May God keep you and save us from the disasters of this war.

Your wife,

Fatima

Gunner William Munton to Nellie Munton

William Munton wrote over 150 letters to his wife during his wartime service, including the letter on pages 27–9 in which he recounts the Christmas he spent 'somewhere in France'. He was a devout Christian, not at ease in a rough male environment, and from his letters it's obvious that he was at odds with most of his fellow soldiers. Perhaps this was why he needed to write so often to the one person who understood him.

It's not clear in this letter exactly what has precipitated the discussion of loose behaviour. Maybe he has been tempted or maybe he's been mocked for being so straitlaced. But clearly something has happened that has rattled him.

Friday March 30/17

My Darling wife

For you are indeed the sweetest Darling in the whole world & when I read your letter today I felt indeed proud to feel that you, who I love more than I can ever say, trusted me so implicitly to always do the right thing. Do you know Nellie Dear, I think that if I were ever tempted & felt myself giving way, the very thought of my dear wife's trust would be sufficient incentive to me, to withstand all evil. I thank

God however, that though the temptations one has to face are very strong, yet I have never felt anything but contempt & revolt for the evils & passions which are indulged in so liberally out here. True, I am one by myself & now that my driver has gone, I am quite on my own with the old lady, all the others are of course in the estaminets, then about three days after payday they are all wanting to borrow money.

Well now Darling, I really don't know what news to send you. I am quite well & getting along quite as well as possible, & that I suppose is the best I can say. I am of course longing to see you again. Ah my Darling, if you only knew how I sit & gaze at your photograph, I don't know what I should do without it. I long and yearn for the time when I shall return to you. Yes, as you say Dear, it is something to thank God for, that we both know each other sufficiently, that we are not in the least anxious or worried concerning the life we are living. Sometimes at night the conversation turns upon life out here and one man will say, 'Well, I promised my wife I would be teetotal out here, but I'm drunk every pay night.' Or another will say 'I promised my mother I wouldn't gamble & she'd go out of her mind if she knew my carryings on.' Or perhaps another will say 'Well I promised my wife I would leave the French mademoiselles alone but I don't' & many similar things are said. Then sometimes I say 'I never promised my wife anything' & someone will say 'No, perhaps she knew you wouldn't.' And I feel deep down in my heart 'That was just it. Thank God she knew.' You have no idea how that thought helps & comforts me. I hope of course that I am living the best life I can & for the best motive, & apart from any home considerations I hope I should still live as I believe God would have me, yet I love you truly Nellie, & when you say what you do in your kind letters, I feel that it is worth repelling all the temptations that come, just for a word of commendation from you. How I treasure some of the things you have so kindly said in your letters, only God & I know. But let me assure you of this My Darling. With the help of God, I shall always live in such a way that I should never be ashamed of any man I meet out here of seeing & knowing me at home, & listening to me preach the gospel of Christ.

I suppose at home, home ties & influences to some extent kept some of these men in bounds, but now freed from all these helps, they find circumstances too strong for them & simply go with the crowd. They haven't to think of going home at night & meeting father or mother, wife or sisters, or any of those things that might make a man ashamed & so gradually they have drifted, until now, when I come with the rations, nearly always the first question I am asked is 'Is there any rum today?' However, Darling, I have drifted into saying this, I certainly never intended to do so, when I started writing.

Well Good Night My Darling & God always Bless you with His richest blessing. Make us, as you often pray, worthy of each other & bring us together soon, in a unity of Love and service for Him.

Give my love to all at home, Lily & Lizzie & the children. Tell Lily to buck up & not to worry – try & keep cheerful &

brave yourself because you know, when I do come home I don't want to find my wife looking aged with worry, I want to find you just as nice & pretty as I left you. God Bless You My Darling & keep you in all things.

With the Best of all Best Love

Your affectionate Husband Will

xxxxxxxxxx

xxxxxxxxxx

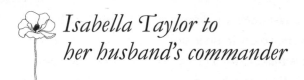

Isabella Taylor to her husband's commander

Nothing is known of the circumstances surrounding this letter, but Isabella Taylor's concern for her husband and her distress is very apparent.

To
The Head Commander of
18 Welsh Reg. A Bey
119 Brigade
40 Division
B.E.F.
France

Jan 28th 1917

Dear Sir

I am writing to asked you if you would be so kind as to look into this matter for me, well it is about my husband, Pte David Taylor 27880 18 Welsh, Reg. Abery, 119 Brigade, 40th Division, I have not had a letter from him for nearly a month, only two Field-cards, to say he as not heard from me for a long time, but Sir, I keep on sending him letters & parcels all the time, but he dont seem to have them, I have sent him a big parcel, 1s 4d for postage, & a small one 7d for postage & this last one it took me over 1s for postage besides letters & papers, so Sir if he is not having them, somebody else is, but it is making my Husband think I dont care about him now he is there but I no I do, it does seem hard on me I can tell you, when I am doing my very best for him all the time, & my little son keeps on asking when is my Daddy coming Mammy, but he as not seen my other baby yet, so Sir if you could look into this for me, it would cheer me up a little, hoping you will oblige

Mrs Isabella Taylor
Cecil Terrace
Chadsmoor
Staffs

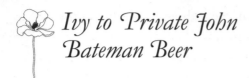

Ivy to Private John Bateman Beer

John Bateman Beer had been serving with a London regiment in Palestine and Egypt since autumn 1916. Far away from home and on active service (he had already been wounded), this letter from his girl back in England must have delivered quite a blow. In a letter to his father, he is philosophical: 'There are far better fish in the sea so I am not going to worry my head about it'. But he isn't completely unaffected by her actions: he's going to 'have a very free & easy time after this war', he writes in the same letter to his father, and not see a woman for 'such a long time'.

Woodfield Cres.
Paddington W9

24/8/17

My Dear Jack,

For the last month I have been endeavouring to pluck up sufficient courage to write and tell you that everything must be over between us. No doubt you will think me awfully unkind and perhaps fickle to write this while you are away, but this matter has worried me a great deal, and I have been halting between two opinions, as to whether it would be kinder to let you know now, and let myself be called unfaithful, or to wait until you come home, although knowing all the time in my heart that I was untrue. When you went away, and I told you that I loved you best, I really meant it Jack, but such a lot seems to have happened since then. I really thought that I had forgotten Charlie in my love for you, and during the past nine months have been fighting against his love for me, wishing and longing for your return, but it is no use Jack, I cannot help loving Charlie best. I suppose it is because he was first. At first I made up my mind to fight it down <u>and be true to you, and if you still wish to keep me to my promise under the circumstances, I will do so.</u>

Don't take this too much to heart Jack. I am not worth it but don't think me altogether heartless. I would not hurt you dear unless I could help it, but unfortunately we cannot control our own feelings. Will you believe me when I say that I am very sorry, for I am, more so than perhaps you think. Anyway, forgive me if you can, and <u>I trust that you will still let us be friends</u>, whatever happens. Have not had the courage to tell your Mother yet, perhaps you will do so. Write back as soon as you can to say you forgive me Jack, shall wait impatiently for your answer.

One word about Charlie before I finish. He would have waited in honour bound until you came home.

All at home send their love to you.

Trusting this will find you in the best of health,

I remain,

Yours Very Sincerely

Ivy

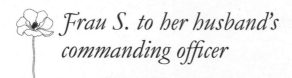

Frau S. to her husband's commanding officer

Frau S. was clearly suffering the absence of her husband greatly when she wrote this letter to his commanding officer. The generous reply suggests he was rather tickled by her request.

Treuen

2 January 1917

Dear Leader of the Company!

I, the signer below, have a request to make of you. Although my husband has only been in the field for four months, I would like to ask you to grant him a leave of absence, namely, because of our sexual relationship. I would like to have my husband just once for the satisfaction of my natural desires. I just can't live like this any more. I can't stand it.

It is, of course, impossible for me to be satisfied in other ways, firstly, because of all the children and secondly, because I do not want to betray my husband. So I would like to ask you very kindly to grant my request. I will then be able to carry on until we are victorious.

With all reverence,

Frau S.

And his reply:

Honourable Frau S!

  With this letter, I confirm the receipt of your friendly letter of 2 January 1917. I can certainly sympathize with you and understand that you would like to see your beloved husband come home, and I will do everything in my power to fulfil your wish. But you must also realize that I have many men in my company at the moment who have been away from their homes for nearly a year. To be fair to these men, I ask you to be patient for another 1-2 weeks. Then, I will be able to add your name to our list of men going on leaves and absences.

  With friendly greetings,
                     K. Zehmisch

2nd Lieutenant Hugh Livingston to Babs Livingston

In the surviving handful of letters this couple exchanged, it is clear that neither of them coped very well with the stress of war. In one letter, Babs Livingston lists the local men (from Low Fell, near Newcastle) who have been recently killed, and tells her husband that her loneliness and anxiety are so great that she has taken to going to bed when it is still daylight. In this letter to Babs, sent from the Front, Hugh Livingston's terrible panic is clearly felt. When his wife reads it, her strain is sure to increase.

B.E.F.
6/10/17

Sweetheart,

One more day in this hellish land has passed over. I wish I could be sitting by your side near our own hearth to be able to tell you what I have seen and been through. I wish I could get an illness or a blighty. The job doesn't suit one of my temperament. I left here (the men) this morning fully expecting not to come through. How men live day after day in the midst of thousands of flying shells is a miracle. I have been in the O.P. today within sight of the Boche lines – have seen a trench strafe and tonight returned through flying shells. You can hear them whistling towards you and wonder when you're going to get one in the neck. However I've pulled through another day. I may pull through them all. This affair makes me think that God sleeps. The only word to describe it is <u>hellish</u>. I've seen aeroplanes coming toppling down head over heels and ghastly things – too ghastly to mention. Now dear, once again, should you never hear again from me, remember I love you and love my little ones. I don't want to make you unhappy, sweetheart, or put the wind up you, but it's as well to face the facts & I never know when the worst may happen day or night. I've seen the spot in the distance where Jack Murray was – you understand?

Heaps of love, darling, to you, treasure, & baby

Your husband ever

Hugh x

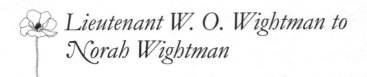

Lieutenant W. O. Wightman to Norah Wightman

William and Norah Wightman conducted their entire relationship, from courtship to marriage, whilst William was in the army and therefore almost permanently absent. His many letters to her are always loving and effusive, until he receives a letter in which she mentions going to a dance and sharing a taxi home with an American officer.

Brussels

Sunday 19 January 1919

My own little girl,

You will hardly be expecting another letter so soon and I have really no news but I am feeling so utterly depressed that it is a relief to my feelings to write to you. Last night I seemed to be awake for hours thinking about you and your Mounthill dance and I couldn't get the Yank Officer out of my mind. And my thoughts resolved themselves into the conclusion that this is a rotten world at the present time. The War has so uprooted things and turned them upside down. People at home seem to have lost their ballast and there seems so little loyalty about people's actions. I think the real tragedies of this War are much more to be found in domestic life at home than out here. After all there is no tragedy about a man giving up his life out here if he dies a gentleman, but it is when one reads of a case like that in the papers now where Colonel Rutherford shot another Officer in his house and I am pretty sure that a good many men at home will be shot when husbands return from France and it will rid the world of some useless creatures.

Darling, when I was thinking about you as I lay awake last night I was wondering what you were wearing, supposing you were at the dance and which of my little presents you might be wearing too. And I wondered if you were wearing the little locket which I gave you in which I wrote 'I love you' which you said you loved to have. And I wondered whether when you were driving alone at night in the car that night, looking the picture of sweetness and purity that you do, you the little wife whom I love and worship, glorious with your wonderful hair and your perfect daintiness all of which I had believed you had dedicated to me alone in return for my love and worship. And as I lay there I wondered if you could realize how you are torturing my feelings, I who am utterly helpless out here. Darling, I know that if you realized you would not do it. But the parting of husbands and wives resulting from husbands being with the forces out here makes life at home for their wives an unnatural existence. But my beloved, we will be together again soon I hope and then let us be as much or more to each other than ever we have been before.

And so do be patient, little love, until I can come home and be your escort and playmate as well as your lover and husband, and do, darling, respect my love and my reasonable wishes and feelings whilst we are to be parted.

Good night, my beloved, and once again, I love and worship you, and do make me your happy husband again and we will have such good times together, my little chummy girl.

Your lover, Billy

Phyllis Kelly to
Private Eric Appleby

Eric Appleby and Phyllis Kelly were experts at imagining what their life would be like when the war was over and they could finally be married. In one of his very last letters to his 'dear one forever', on pages 87–9, the thought of being with her for just one weekend exhilarated and sustained him.

Here Phyllis writes to her 'darling Englishman' immediately after hearing the news that he has been seriously wounded. Her shock and utter desperation ring true in every single word.

Unposted letter

28 October 1916

My own darling Englishman,

I wonder why I'm writing this, which you may never see – oh God, perhaps even now you have gone far away from your Lady – I wonder when another telegram will come; this knowing nothing is terrible, I don't know what to do. I simply have sat and shivered since your dad's wire came. It was forwarded from Athlone to Pembroke Road as that was the address we had given the post office. Mum brought it to Leeson Street. I was in my room unpacking and had just hung up 'Eric' over my bed, when the old maid came up to tell me Mum was downstairs and down I rushed. That anything was the matter never occurred to me until I saw her face. Oh my love, my love, what shall I do – but I must be brave and believe all will be well – dear one, surely God won't take you from me now. It will be the end of everything that matters because, oh Englishman, you are all the world and life to me. But I must be brave like you, dear, but the words of your dad's telegram will keep ringing in my head and squashing out hope. 'Dangerously wounded'. I say it over and over again till it doesn't seem to mean anything – when I came over to Pembroke Road with Mum, I tried very hard to pray but no words will come into my head, except 'Oh God, give him back to me.' This writing to you is the only thing that makes the waiting easier – everybody is very kind, I know, but I feel I would give anything to be by myself – I think I will go to Leeson Street now to see if there is another wire.

31 October, from Eric's father to Phyllis's mother

'Wire just received Eric died of wounds Saturday heard nothing more'

*Phyllis never married and kept Eric's picture
above her bed for the rest of her life.*

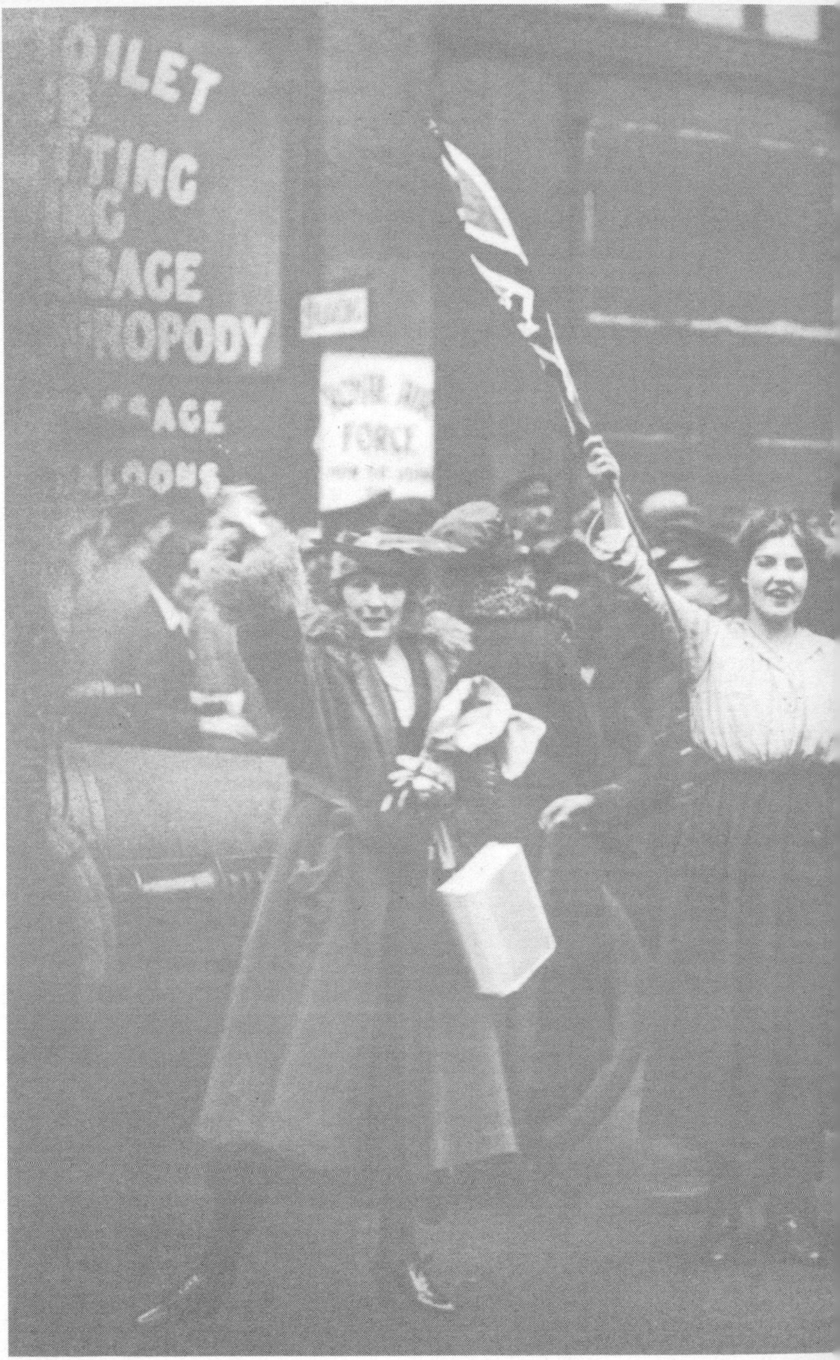
ILET
TING
SAGE
ROPODY
AGE
FORCE

VIII. THE END OF THE WAR

So fundamental had letter-writing become in wartime that it wasn't unusual for wives and sweethearts to continue to write letters, unposted, to their men killed on the battlefield. But for the lucky ones, pen and paper could now be put aside and life could begin again.

Agnes von Kurowsky to Ernest Hemingway

In 1918, eighteen-year-old Ernest Hemingway served as an ambulance driver on the Italian Front. In July that year he sustained serious shrapnel wounds in both legs, and was sent to recuperate in a Milan hospital. There he met Agnes von Kurowsky, a twenty-six-year-old American nurse, and fell in love with her. By the time he had recovered and was ready to return to America in 1919, they had decided to marry. Then Hemingway received the following letter.

In A Farewell to Arms, his novel set during the Italian campaign of the First World War, the character Catherine Barkley, a nurse, was inspired by Agnes.

Ernie, dear boy,

I am writing this late at night after a long think by myself, & I am afraid it is going to hurt you, but, I'm sure it won't harm you permanently.

For quite a while before you left, I was trying to convince myself it was a real love-affair, because, we always seemed to disagree, & then arguments always wore me out so that I finally gave in to keep you from doing something desperate.

Now, after a couple of months away from you, I know that I am still very fond of you, but, it is more as a mother than as a sweetheart. It's alright to say I'm a Kid, but, I'm not, & I'm getting less & less so every day.

So, Kid (still Kid to me, & always will be) can you forgive me some day for unwittingly deceiving you? You know I'm not really bad, & don't mean to do wrong, & now I realize it was my fault in the beginning that you cared for me, & regret it from the bottom of my heart. But, I am now & always will be too old, & that's the truth, & I can't get away from the fact that you're just a boy – a kid.

I somehow feel that some day I'll have reason to be proud of you, but, dear boy, I can't wait for that day, & it was wrong to hurry a career.

I tried hard to make you understand a bit of what I was thinking on that trip from Padua to Milan, but, you acted like a spoiled child, & I couldn't keep on hurting you. Now, I only have the courage because I'm far away.

Then – & believe me when I say this is sudden for me, too – I expect to be married soon. And I hope & pray that after you thought things out, you'll be able to forgive me & start a wonderful career & show what a man you really are.

Ever admiringly & fondly,
Your friend,
      Aggie

Phyllis Iliff to
Lieutenant Philip Pemble

This young couple had known each other since school. Philip was nineteen years old, Phyllis only seventeen. He had been in the air force only a few months when he was killed over Dunkirk in June 1918. Eight months later Phyllis prepared what she called a Memorial Book, in which she wrote poetry and letters to him. This is the first letter. Its occasional melodramatic note reminds us that Phyllis was very young and that she would get over her sorrow (and indeed she did, marrying a few years later), but this doesn't diminish the intensity of her grief.

My own dearest darling Phil,

And so after all this is the end, you who were so certain of coming back & I who was so certain of it too, have to own ourselves completely baffled.

On that beautiful Saturday morning your life went out 'into the ether' – and you left me here!

From higher than the highest hill you come spinning down. Your body, which should have belonged to me, must have made a big hole in the ground. And I, who could have made life beautiful for you even though you would have been crippled, or disfigured or blind, may not touch, or hear, or see you any more. My useless tears are falling.

I cannot believe that life – the abundant share of it which was yours – could finish so utterly, or that the individuality which made you mine, could go back into nothingness again.

Last night in the darkness I lay & realized what it means to be alone. No one will ever understand me as you did. People try, but it always ends in 'Blessed if I can make you out, kid!' or 'Hang it, Phyl, I can't understand you in the least.' There are one or two who say 'Perhaps I understand you better than you do yourself' & these don't understand me one little bit.

Heaps of people say they love me but what is love without understanding? – nothing, I realized also how completely my life ended when yours did. Oh! I wish Death would hurry & come this way! One extra wouldn't make much difference to him when he takes crowds and crowds.

I went to church last Sunday, Phil dear, but when the preacher got up and started telling me how wonderful God was, I had an awful desire to stand up and say 'Is God like Phil?' Wouldn't the people have been surprised if I had?

It has been snowing here for the last day or so & on the other afternoon I climbed right up to the top of the house & looked out over a white, white world, but instead of seeing all the roofs covered with snow I saw just one little grave far away in a French cemetery with a plain wooden cross at the head & your dear name inscribed thereon.

The other day at the shop one of the girls asked when my 'boy' was coming home & as I did not answer another one said 'Miss Iliff doesn't like boys, do you, Miss Iliff?' I felt so awful I just got up & went out of the room & into the dark stockroom & there among the darkness & dust I cried & cried for about ten minutes and then I slipped down into the shop & round to the cloakroom & washed the remains of my tears away & powdered my nose & I went down to face the criticisms of the girls. No one has ever said anything to me about that evening, but they must have thought I was pretty far gone! Oh! thank God none of these have ever had cause to feel like I did & I sincerely hope they never may.

I really must leave off now, darling, as it is nearly tea time. If ever I get married I shall burn this book, your dear letters & your still dearer photos on the eve of my wedding day & go forth on my new life with only your glorious memory to help.

All my love, dear one,
Phyl

Hanna von Reuter to Rear Admiral Ludwig von Reuter (Herzel)

Ludwig von Reuter's battleship, the SMS Emden, *had been captured by the British forces and, along with the rest of the surrendered German fleet, was anchored at Scapa Flow in the Orkney Islands, awaiting its fate. This had been the situation for nine months, and Hanna was despairing. But within a week her misery turns to joy – and it's impossible not to feel glad for her at such happiness and relief. At first, the roses are 'not up to much' but by the end, when she knows he's coming home, 'The roses are lasting as never before, dark red, every day I bring a whole basket in; when you come, everything is to be full of roses.'*

Wilhelmshaven, 14.6.19

My beloved darling,

I am so unhappy, Fräulein Grete has just come in as white as a sheet – all our chicks are lying dead in the coop – today they were just 3 weeks old and were so chubby and lively, it was a joy to look at them every day. It's such a shame. I wonder if they've eaten something? I don't know. The day before yesterday we put in another brood-hen, no chicks. In the garden the weeds are rampant, more than ever, our potatoes are miserable and everything else is weeds. There's no doubt they cheated me with the seed-potatoes. The sparrows have eaten the peas, there's scarcely anything left. Now the roses are beginning to flower but as they weren't pruned they're not up to much either. As you can see, I have my worries. The warm weather has gone again, instead there are storms or rain and it's cold. My darling, I hope that during the next week the decision will be made about the peace settlement. Will you soon be with me again at last?

Evening. Just back from Wicht, Gosorek was there too. My darling, I could weep, if only I had you back again. I long for you, just as you do for me. Do come back, and let me kiss you long and lovingly. I live only in my thoughts of you, that you will be with me again. But, darling, your letters worry me, what's the matter with you? You say I should go to Ali or Ernst when I'm anxious about you – darling, what does that mean? If only you were with me. I long for you, for your love and care. I am beside myself. Are you not all right? Oh darling, darling, what's the matter? Come back to me, to me and the boys, that's the only place where you belong, we need you, need you desperately. What more do you want to do over there? Everything is past saving, why sacrifice yourself for nothing?

Sunday, 15.6

How many Sundays I have spent without you! It's really no pleasure, I miss you so much, you know I don't care about other people, but you I miss, I need one other person to be wholly mine, oh my darling when are you coming back? I am in complete agreement with your resigning, and wouldn't delay, I think you've done more than your duty; it might be different if there were any prospects of a job later, but there's nothing doing. So it's more sensible to look around for something else more positive. I feel so strongly that you with your abilities which are far above the average could find some better use for them. Our ships are gone – the government hasn't an atom of interest for the navy. You're fighting for a lost cause. It is of no help, either to yourself or your country, and merely to stand by your post because there's nobody else? No, you're too good for that.

Monday, 16.9

Herzel my darling, my hand and heart are trembling with joy. Just as I was about to sit down and write to you again Blanquet telephones – you have asked to be relieved and there is some hope that you will be here next week. Oh my darling, I will hardly be able to wait. I am glad, so glad. I want you here at once, immediately.

20.6.19

My darling, my thoughts are only, when are you coming, when will you be with me at last? Inside I am totally kaputt, I can't take any more, I could weep, but with you I shall laugh, my darling, have no fear, we two will make progress in life, 'how' will become clear somehow. Yesterday I picked the first strawberries, I hope you will be back in time to eat some with us. The roses are lasting as never before, dark red, every day I bring a whole basket in; when you come, everything is to be full of roses. My darling, I hope you will come next week in the cruiser, actually I'm counting on it; then I shall forget everything in your arms, hear nothing, see nothing, except you alone.

With love, your Hanna

This letter and the one on pages 40–1 from Maria to Anselm Lautenschlager – who served on the Emden *alongside von Reuter – never reached their destination. We don't really know why this was so, but perhaps delivering post to the captured German fleet was not a priority at that time. The letters did reach Britain, however, and are in the Liddle Collection at the University of Leeds in the file of a Royal Navy lieutenant who served at Scapa Flow in 1919. They remained unopened until 1989, when they were donated to the Collection. Perhaps the lieutenant had always meant to send them on, or maybe he simply forgot about them. It seems a shame such beautiful love letters never reached those they were intended for.*

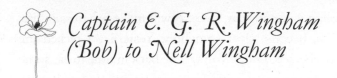

Captain E. G. R. Wingham (Bob) to Nell Wingham

Bob Wingham could have written an ecstatic and excited long letter to his wife, as he reports to her that he is at long last coming home from service in Egypt. Instead, he keeps it short and sweet, but it is no less memorable for that.

Leitoun

Sat night 9 p.m.

11.1.19

My little Nell-wife,

This is the very last letter to be written to you from Leitoun from your Bob-husband, for he leaves here tomorrow morning by the 9.22 train from Leitoun. At Cairo main station, I catch the 11 am train to Kantara – on the Suez Canal – near Port Said. My kit is packed & includes several things for the Nell. I shall with luck be home by the end of the month, but I am travelling on duty as I have received orders to act in England as a Demobilizing Officer.

I shall probably be home as soon as, or very soon after, this letter is delivered. So after all, little girl of mine, I am to see the little house you have found for us. Can you realize what a happy Bob it is this Sat. night who quite soon knows he will be at home with his Nell? I want you to be glad I am coming home & want you to be very pleased to see me again. I am coming home to make us prosperous & you are going to help me forget some of the frightfulness of these last four years.

Goodnight dearest Nell-wife

From the Bob

Private Horace Humpage to Patty Hignett

Horace Humpage's proposal of marriage to Patty Hignett at the end of the war seems a little unromantic and matter-of-fact, and one could be forgiven for assuming that he has simply been caught up in Armistice wedding fever. But he admits he has difficulty putting his feelings into words and adds thirty-six kisses to compensate.

And he did mean it: Horace and Patty married eighteen months later in May 1920, and were together for nearly sixty years.

Dec 5th 18

Dear Patty

Just a few lines to thank you for a letter rec. a few days ago. I hope you have quite got over your flu.

Well I must apologize to you for I have not been able to write lately however it won't occur again.

I am going to Bethlehem today to get a few things for home so if I see anything new I will get something for you.

Well Patty I'm going to talk serious to you something like a Dutch Uncle sort of style. I think that we have known each other long enough now to come to some definite arrangement. I suppose that some day or other I shall be coming home and I think that when I get settled I would like to get married. I'm afraid I'm not one at putting it very well but I think for your sake that is if you think the same way as I do that we ought to get engaged. I suppose that's the proper way so let me know what you think. I think you know what I am and pretty well all about me and if you decide my way I will do my best to make you a good husband and a comfortable home. If you do, I suppose I should buy you an engagement ring so if you will have a look at some and will tell me the price I will send you the money for it.

Patty don't be frightened to tell me what you think and let me know there's a dear.

Yours

Horace

xxxxxxxxxxxx

xxxxxxxxxxxx

xxxxxxxxxxxx

Rudolf Sauter to his sweetheart

*Rudolf Sauter was in an internment camp at Alexandra Palace,
London, for the entire duration of the war. He was German, his
sweetheart English. The end of the war was bittersweet for them.
He could now be released but he would have to leave England
(where he had made his home): anti-German feeling would have
made it impossible for him to stay.*

Nov 6–13, 1918
Alexandra Palace

My Own Loved One . . .

It is so wonderful to know that my letters mean much to
you, that they can help things a little over this time, when we
cannot be together, except in Spirit and with the beating of
our hearts. It comes to me often that these written thoughts
must be so little use, they seem so cold, such a very poor
reflection of all that I want to speak to you. But in them you
must always read what I can never find the words to say. I
think the hand writes much that thought would leave unsaid
and fails directly it is confronted by the great things of the
soul.

And now: for the days which pass us by so filled with great
events that we can hardly begin to realize their significance.

Here most are in a great state of nerves. For their distraction people turn to patience and it is not an uncommon sight (up here in the Tower) to see as many as 11 intelligent businessmen, in full possession of all their faculties playing patience at one time, ensconced in all corners and tables of the room. It gives one almost the impression of a mad house. Thus they try to fight their thoughts, their sorrow, their fears and bitterness with any kind of triviality.

I have just read the armistice conditions!! Yes, my Darling, they are hard for <u>any</u> people to bear; and if the peace conditions which follow are equally so, then, firstly one sees the real 'ideals' for which the money-grabbing lawyers of the twenty-three nations have been fighting and secondly, another war, the child of this very day, like a ghost, haunting the future! You see, here one is living among the defeated. And, whether they feel more patriotism or less, whether they are much or little attached to their native country matters little at this moment. These men here chose England for their home, most of them now feel how impossible it will be to live here afterwards. Most have suffered much through their enforced captivity amongst unnatural surroundings; they have been parted from their families, their businesses have, in many cases, disappeared as in a quicksand and now they are about to be turned out into a world already made poor enough by war. How many of these, whom this life has narrowed and embittered, can see in armistice – the end of organized murder – the beginning of the pipes of spring. And ignore victory or defeat as incidental, only, to the growth of mankind and the birth of the conception of a wider humanity. Only dreamers of dreams!

Peace, at last, Darling! – think what it means after all these years of suffering. It seems so strange to be at peace, as it was at first unrealizable to be at war. I cannot yet grasp the idea properly.

And now, my own Sweet Soul, comes that great question, to which (should it arise) one must have an answer ready:– what do you feel is my duty, what do you feel is best? That I should go straight over to Germany, when the time comes to be released, or to make special application to be allowed to stay here, arrange about the house etc until things are sufficiently settled for Mother and me to go over together? We have both agreed that it would, in any case, be necessary to go sometime, rather than to try and stay here permanently, haven't we? You know how much I long to be with my <u>loved</u> One. To go, will not be easy. Yet, if the parting has to come – this short parting, till I have learnt a little more, worked for you and made some headway up towards our dreams – is it not better, that it should come soon, that the sooner I may be able to win a place for you, learn to be worthy of your beautiful Spirit, until I may ask . . . Oh, my Darling, you know . . . Yes! I know how hard it will be for you – to wait, to wait . . . as hard as your love is great and strong and wonderful. But it will not be for long in any case. What, then, do you feel is right? Last time you asked me what was the matter . . . but, without any answer, you knew what was in my thoughts.

Oh; these talks with you must always come to an unfinished end, a sudden breaking off for time always steals close and tears away the minutes, before I can say one half of all I want to talk with you about. Now I must hurry! Do not let this letter make you unhappy – these things we have to face sometime and each must learn to see in the sadness of others some place where help from him may lighten them . . .

All, all my love! that is near and about you wherever you are. Love knows no distance, time is ours and Beauty finds no breaking-shore . . .

R

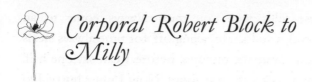

Corporal Robert Block to Milly

Robert Block wrote this joyous letter to his sweetheart on the day after peace was declared.

12 November 1918

Dear Darling Milly,

Although I hardly know what to write, I feel quietly pleased and complacent. All night I was thinking of you and my self and – ah – all the world. We heard it yesterday evening – 'All hostilities have ceased.' My Dear Heart, I do believe you and all at home have been praying for our return. Millie, my heart is too full all since last night to write that letter which I want to . . .

Dearest, do you remember that letter you sent me. The one with your first photo. Oh yes, girl, I still have it and it holds too a small ring of hair and a small photo of Napoleon. I told you that that small curl of hair would be with me. And the other, well, humour it, a whim, Napoleon could not get to Jerusalem so I carried his likeness through for him, that's all. Oh I am quite sane. You see the state of our mental balance because – well Egypt is Egypt and the sun is very hot. Well, Dearest, let us get back to ourselves.

In that letter you also say, 'I shall soon be with you so

where's the odds'. Please God ever so soon, Millie darling, I am hoping and praying for good times for us now. I was thinking of building a hermit's hut at Stonehenge so as to forget the Army and never run into a soldier, or see the flash of brass button. Oh well, Millie, what possibilities we can now look forward to. Millie Darling, I have always wanted you; and now I want you ever so much more. Why have you let people make you believe that the world is so one-sided. At first it was all roses and music. Later, you feel the thorns and discord. Blend all four and you get the maximum of joy that the world has to offer. Anyway, I am all out for the roses and music proposition now. Millie, can you tell me this; why it is a chap wants to sit in a quiet corner and have a think, this eternally happens. Someone sits down at the piano and tears the chap's heart and soul to pieces with a sweet melody sacred to the listener's heart and soul. Darling, do you remember one Saturday night just before we sat down to a quiet tea, it was in your place and you were holding your baby sister and crooning over her. Suddenly you looked up and asked, 'Bobby, how much do you love me?'

I replied, 'I don't know.' And your eyes opened wide and searched my face. You dropped your head over the baby and softly sang 'Roses of Picardy'. I wonder if you understood my answer. You must have done, for you sang that song ever so nice. And last night just before the news came through, I heard a chap play 'Roses of Picardy' and if you did not come and stand before me I saw you smile and was glad for that. And outside down the docks I heard the ships' sirens and softly blessed them because they spelt you and all in this world to me. Now a chap can't be ratty with another chap for playing a piano if the player is good and the tunes those which soothe as roses and prick as thorns. So I pictured you bending over that kid and I loved 'Roses of Picardy' because I love you. But there it is, one moment you are chasing Turks with a little more than friendly interest, the next you go to butter because a chap plays a tune when you feel lonely. Now every boy bad as beer and every girl ditto, we have a few, have at times the emotions of saints. So the old world is not so bad after all. Only as I once said before; people are apt to look at the world through dirty windows. Well, Millie everything is balanced for us so we can't grouse. I don't feel exactly like laughing even now. Only I pray to God to give us both all that we hope and pray for. Millie Darling, Oh I do so love you and want you but I must wait just a little longer I suppose. If I only get across the Mediterranean Sea it would not be so bad. On the right side of Egypt then. Was it Raleigh or Drake who kissed the stones of Plymouth quay when he landed. Funny, if a chap did it in our enlightened age he would hear 'Poor chap, been in Egypt, y'know.' Mill girl, I am going to smile if I crack the only glass our tent possesses.

Yours, Bob

'Roses of Picardy', the song that made Corporal Robert Block 'go to butter' when he heard it being played on the night peace was declared, was one of the most popular songs of the war. It was written in 1916 by Fred E. Weatherly and set to music by Haydn Wood. Robert Block described the tune as one of those 'which soothe as roses and prick as thorns', a perfect description of its lovely, aching melancholy.

Roses of Picardy

She is watching by the poplars,
Colinette with the sea blue eyes
She is watching and longing and waiting
Where the long white roadway lies.
And a song stirs in the silence,
As the wind in the boughs above
She listens and starts and trembles
'Tis the first little song of love.

Roses are shining in Picardy
In the hush of the silver dew
Roses are flow'ring in Picardy
But there's never a rose like you!
And the roses will die with the summer time
And our roads may be far apart
But there's one rose that dies not in Picardy
'Tis the rose that I keep in my heart!

And the years fly on forever
Till their shadows veil their skies
But he loves to hold her little hands
And look in her sea blue eyes.
And she sees the road by the poplars
Where they met in the bygone years
For the first little song of the roses
Is the last little song she hears.

Roses are shining in Picardy
In the hush of the silver dew
Roses are flow'ring in Picardy
But there's never a rose like you!
And the roses will die with the summer time
And our roads may be far apart
But there's one rose that dies not in Picardy
'Tis the rose that I keep in my heart!

Acknowledgements

Grateful thanks must go to Tom Walker for his advice and enthusiasm, Juliet Chalk for her French translations and Richard Davies at the Liddle Collection for his invaluable help.

Thanks also to the Imperial War Museums (Documents and Sound Section) and the Liddle Collection at the Brotherton Library at the University of Leeds for allowing access to their collections, and to the copyright holders for permission to publish, including Simon Chater, Arthur Stockwin, Jan Timson, Julian S. Maslin, Phyllis M. Wells, Doreen Priddey, Henry Sanford, Andrew Sherwin, Roy Galbraith, Susan Overton, Yvonne Long, J. E. Overall, Belinda Lee-Jones and Ann Humpage.

Source Notes and Credits

ABBREVIATIONS

IWM Imperial War Museums
AWM Australian War Memorial

Where appropriate, we have made every effort to acknowledge copyright holders, and the author, the Liddle Collection and the Imperial War Museum would be grateful for any information which might help to trace those whose identities or addresses are not currently known.

I. CHEERO, BLUE EYES

Corporal Alfred Chater to Joyce Francis, 25 October 1914: Private Papers (1697), IWM.
Lieutenant Geoffrey Boothby to Edith Ainscow, 26 July 1915: *Thirty-odd Feet Below Belgium: An Affair of Letters in the Great War*, 1915–16, ed. Arthur Stockwin, Parapress, 2005.
Lieutenant Erwin von Freiherr Pflanzer-Baltin to Violet Murchison, 3 August 1914. Private Papers (GE24), Liddle Collection.
Private Thomas Hughes to his wife, 8/9 September 1914: Durham Light Infantry Museum.

Sergeant Major Giuseppe Castellani to Antonia Castellani, 19 September
1917: Europeana 1914–18; www.europeana1914-18.eu.
Contributed by Manuel Castellani.
Herbert Weisser to his sweetheart: German Students' War Letters, ed.
Philipp Witkop, trans. A. F. Wedd, Pine Street Books, 2002.
Private Wellington Murray Dennis to Margaret Munro, 4 May 1917: The
Canadian Letters and Images Project; www.canadianletters.ca.
From Private Vasily Mishnin's Diary, 25 December 1915: Private
collection Alexandra Mishnin. Extract trans. Helen Ferguson,
quoted in *A War in Words*, Svetlana Palmer and Sarah Wallis,
Simon & Schuster, 2003.
Dick to Molly: quoted in 'My Diary of the Great War to Nov
1916', Pat McCormick, IWM.

II. SOMEWHERE IN FRANCE

Gunner William Munton to Nellie Munton, 26 December 1916:
Private Papers (15315), IWM.
Gunner Wilfrid Cove to Ethel Cove, 14–15 November 1916; *Wilfrid
to Marjorie*, 4 December 1916: Private Papers (GS0375), Liddle
Collection.
Private Roscoe C. Chittim to Vera Diamond Chittim, 6 November
1918: Private Collection, Tuleta Boatman Spellman. Quoted in
'A Million Kisses: Love Letters from a Doughboy in France',
Paul N. Spellman, *Southwestern Historical Quarterly*, Vol. 114,
No. 1, July 2010.
Maria to Lieutenant Commander Anselm Lautenschlager, 31 May 1919:
Private Papers (GE31), Liddle Collection.
Private James Davies to May, 14 November 1917: Private Papers
(15106), IWM.
Private Guillaume Apollinaire to Madeleine Pagès, 11 October 1915:
An extract from the original letter, published in Guillaume

Apollinaire, *Letters to Madeline*, pp309-15 © Seagull Books, 2010. English translation © Donald Nicholson-Smith. Translated from *Lettres à Madeleine: Tendre comme le souvenir.* Augmented and revised edition, edited by Laurence Campa © Editions Gallimard, Paris, 2005.

Rifleman Bert Bailey to Lucilla Bailey, 27 October 1915: quoted in *1914–18: Voices and Images of the Great War*, Lyn Macdonald, Michael Joseph, 1988.

Edward Marcellus to Goldie Marcellus: Private Collection © Richard E. Leggee. Quoted in *War Letters: Extraordinary Correspondence from American Wars*, ed. Andrew Carroll, Scribner, 2001.

III. SEPARATION AND LONGING

To Dafadar Prayag Singh from his wife, 20 February 1917: © Crown copyright. India Office Records, British Library.

A conscientious objector to his wife: Private Papers (C0099), Liddle Collection.

Lieutenant Roland Leighton to Vera Brittain, 26 August 1915: Vera Brittain archive, William Ready Division of Archives and Research Collections, McMaster University Library.

Mary Corfield to Captain Frederick Corfield, 17 March 1917: Private Papers (GS0365), Liddle Collection.

Marthe Gylbert to an unknown Australian soldier, 25 August 1918: AWM PR03970.

Lance Corporal Walter Williamson to Amelia Williamson, 21 May 1918: Estate of Walter Williamson. *From A Tommy at Ypres, Walter's War: The Diary and Letters of Walter Williamson*, ed. Doreen Priddey, Amberley Publishing, 2011.

Christl Wolf to 1st Lieutenant Leopold Wolf (Poldi), 11 May 1918: Translation Copyright © Shaun Whiteside. Quoted in Christa Hämmerle, "'You let a weeping woman call you home?"

Private correspondences during the First World War in Austria and Germany', from *Epistolary Selves: Letters and Letter-writers, 1600–1945*, pp. 152–82, ed. Rebecca Earle, Ashgate Press Ltd, 1999. The Christl and Leopold Wolf Correspondence is kept in the Sammlung Frauennachlässe (Collection of Women's Personal Papers), NL 14 I, University of Vienna.

Captain W. D. Darling to Bee Darling, 22 January 1918: Private Papers (3472), IWM.

Private Marcel Rivier to Louise Rivier, October 1914: Translation Copyright © Juliet Chalk. Original letter quoted in *Paroles de Poilus: Lettres et Carnets du Front, 1914–1918*, ed. Jean-Pierre Guéno and Yves Laplume, Librio, 1998.

Captain J. S. D. Berrington to his wife, 7 June 1916: Private Papers (16660), IWM.

Private Paul Hub to Maria Thumm, 26 April 1917: translated by Sabine Pusch, quoted in *A War in Words*, Svetlana Palmer and Sarah Wallis, Simon & Schuster, 2003. The Correspondence of Paul Hub is kept in the Hauptstaatsarchiv, Stuttgart.

2nd Lieutenant Clifford Vincent to Iris Dutton, 1 September 1917: Private Papers (GS1657), Liddle Collection.

Amy Handley to Private John George Clifton: July/August 1918: Private Papers (GS0330), Liddle Collection.

IV. APRÈS LA GUERRE

Private Eric Appleby to Phyllis Kelly, 17 October 1916: *Love Letters from the Front: Letters from Eric Appleby to Phyllis Kelly*, ed. Jean Kelly, Marino Books, 2000. Reprinted with kind permission.

An anonymous woman to Private George Bagshaw, 22 April 1919: Private Papers (GS0070), Liddle Collection.

Agnes Miller to Olaf Stapledon, 21 April 1918: © J. D. Stapledon and

Mary S. Shenai. Quoted in *Talking Across the World: The Love Letters of Olaf Stapledon and Agnes Miller, 1913–1919*, ed. Robert Crossley, University Press of New England, 1987.

Ethel Gawthorp to Private Walter C. Shaw, 1 July 1916: Private Papers (GS1447), Liddle Collection.

V. SILVER LININGS

2nd Lieutenant Francis M. Tracy to Gertrude Tracy, 20 September 1918: Private Collection © Christina Wise-Mohr. Quoted in *War Letters: Extraordinary Correspondence from American Wars*, ed. Andrew Carroll, Scribner, 2001.

Private James Riddell to Nurse Cynthia Kennedy: Private Papers (DF075), Liddle Collection.

Captain Alfred Bland to Violet Bland, 1916: With kind permission of the family.

Nurse Betty Robinson to Private Robert Galbraith, 1917: Private Papers (17031), IWM.

Private Marin Guillaumont to Marguerite Guillaumont, December 1914: Translation Copyright © Juliet Chalk. Original letter quoted in *Paroles de Poilus: Lettres et Carnets du Front, 1914–1918*, ed. Jean-Pierre Guéno and Yves Laplume, Librio, 1998.

Dora Willatt to 2nd Lieutenant Cecil Slack, 7 June 1916, and his reply: © Sir William Willatt Slack and the Slack family.

Helen Muriel Harpin to 2nd Lieutenant Charles L. Overton, 3 October 1918: Private Papers (3051), IWM.

Cicely Marriott to Colonel Sidney Marriott, 6 August 1915: Private Papers (GS1052), Liddle Collection.

From Edith Airey's autograph book: quoted in *The Virago Book of Women and the Great War*, ed. Joyce Marlow, 1999.

VI. THE LONGEST GOODBYE

Winston Churchill to Clementine Churchill, 17 July 1915: Reproduced with permission of Curtis Brown, London on behalf of the Estate of Sir Winston Churchill. Copyright © Winston S. Churchill.

Private Lazare Silbermann to Sally Silbermann, 7 August 1914: Translation Copyright © Juliet Chalk. Original letter quoted in *Paroles de Poilus: Lettres et Carnets du Front, 1914–1918*, ed. Jean-Pierre Guéno and Yves Laplume, Librio, 1998.

Captain John Coull to Fred Coull, 2 April 1917: quoted in *Despatches from the Heart: An Anthology of Letters from the Front*, ed. Annette Tapert, Hamish Hamilton, 1984.

Gunner Frank Bracey to Win, 5 May 1916: Private Papers (2895), IWM.

Sergeant Francis Gautier to Marie Gautier, 2 April 1916: Private Papers (2296), IWM.

VII. DARK DAYS

Thomas Rentoul to Ivy, 9 December 1916: Noni Faragher, ed. *Prelude, Fugue and Variations: Letters to a Loved One from Chaplain T. C. Rentoul in World War One*, Spectrum Publications, 1989.

A wife to her husband, a prisoner of war, April 1917: Quoted in *German Soldiers in the Great War: Letters and Eyewitness Accounts*, eds. Bernd Ulrich and Benjamin Ziemann, Pen and Sword Military, 2010.

Private Maurice Drans to Georgette Clabault, 17 May 1917: Translation Copyright © Juliet Chalk. Original letter quoted in *Paroles de Poilus: Lettres et Carnets du Front, 1914–1918*, ed. Jean-Pierre Guéno and Yves Laplume, Librio, 1998.

2nd Lieutenant Stanley Huntington to Coralie, 16 December 1917:

Private Papers (Anzac/NZ/S. H. Huntington), Liddle
Collection.

Emily Chitticks to Private William Martin, 29 March 1917: Private
Papers (2554), IWM.

A Turkish wife to her husband: Quoted in *War Letters: Extraordinary
Correspondence from American Wars*, ed. Andrew Carroll,
Scribner, 2001.

Gunner William Munton to Nellie Munton: Private Papers (15315), IWM.

Isabella Taylor to her husband's commander, 28 January 1917: Private
Papers Captain B. D. Gibbs (12816), IWM.

Ivy to Private John Bateman Beer, 24 August 1917: Private Papers
(2295), IWM.

Frau S. to her husband's commanding officer, 2 January 1917, and his
reply: Collection in Flanders Fields Museum, Ieper.

2nd Lieutenant Hugh Livingston to Babs Livingston, 6 October 1917:
Private Papers (GS0971), Liddle Collection.

Lieutenant W. O. Wightman to Norah Wightman, 19 January 1919:
Private Papers (11644), IWM.

Phyllis Kelly to Private Eric Appleby, 28 October 1916, and the
telegram from Eric's father to Phyllis's mother, 31 October
1916: *Love Letters from the Front: Letters from Eric Appleby to
Phyllis Kelly*, ed. Jean Kelly, Marino Books, 2000. Reprinted
with kind permission.

VIII. THE END OF THE WAR

Agnes von Kurowsky to Ernest Hemingway, 7 March 1919: Quoted in
Hemingway in Love and War: the Lost Diary of Agnes von Kurowsky,
eds. Henry Villard and James Nagel, University Press of New
England, Lebanon, NH, 1989. Reprinted with permission.

Phyllis Iliff to Lieutenant Philip Pemble, 2 February 1919: Private
Papers (DF069), Liddle Collection.

Hanna von Reuter to Rear Admiral Ludwig von Reuter, 14–20 June
  1919: Private Papers (GE30), Liddle Collection.

Captain E.G.R. Wingham to Nell Wingham, 11 January 1919: Private
  Papers (GS1772), Liddle Collection.

Private Horace Humpage to Patty Hignett, 5 December 1918: Private
  Papers (EP038), Liddle Collection.

Rudolf Sauter to his sweetheart, 6–13 November 1918: Private Papers
  (8056), IWM.

Corporal Robert Block to Milly, 12 November 1918: Private Papers
  (11939), IWM.

'Roses of Picardy': Lyrics by Frederick Weatherly. Music by
  Haydn Wood. Sheet music, Chappell & Co., London, 1916.